WHERE THE WATER GOES AROUND

WHERE THE WATER GOES AROUND

Beloved Detroit

≈

Bill Wylie-Kellermann
FOREWORD BY *Gloria House*

CASCADE *Books* · Eugene, Oregon

WHERE THE WATER GOES AROUND
Beloved Detroit

Copyright © 2017 Bill Wylie-Kellermann. All rights reserved. Except for brief quotations in critical publications or reviews, no part of this book may be reproduced in any manner without prior written permission from the publisher. Write: Permissions, Wipf and Stock Publishers, 199 W. 8th Ave., Suite 3, Eugene, OR 97401.

Cascade Books
An Imprint of Wipf and Stock Publishers
199 W. 8th Ave., Suite 3
Eugene, OR 97401

www.wipfandstock.com

PAPERBACK ISBN: 978-1-4982-9649-6
HARDCOVER ISBN: 978-1-4982-9651-9
EBOOK ISBN: 978-1-4982-9650-2

Cataloguing-in-Publication data:

Names: Wylie-Kellermann, Bill. | foreword by Gloria House.

Title: Where the water goes around : beloved Detroit / Bill Wylie-Kellermann.

Description: Eugene, OR: Cascade Books, 2017 | Includes bibliographical references and index.

Identifiers: ISBN 978-1-4982-9649-6 (paperback) | ISBN 978-1-4982-9651-9 (hardcover) | ISBN 978-1-4982-9650-2 (ebook)

Subjects: LCSH: 1. Detroit (Mich.) Economic conditions. | 2. Detroit (Mich.) Social conditions. | 3. Theology. | I. Title.

Classification: HC108.06 W500 2017 (print) | HC108 (ebook)

Manufactured in the U.S.A.   JULY 3, 2017

Special permission granted to use the following articles from *Sojourners Magazine*

"Discerning the Angel of Detroit: The Spirits and Powers at Work in One City," October 1989

"Readers Before Profits," January/February, 1996

"Resurrection City: How Detroit Comes Alive in the New Depression," May 2009

All reprinted with permission from Sojourners, (800) 714-7474, www.sojo.net.

For Charity Hicks,
Waging love with the Ancestors

Contents

Acknowledgements xi
Cover Story xvii
Foreword – Gloria House xix
Introduction xxiii

1989
Discerning the Angel of Detroit:
   The Spirits and Powers at Work in One City 1

1992
Stations of the Cross 13
   Introduction 13
   Station: The Detroit River 15
   Station: Casinos 16

1994
City Life, Scenes and Feelings:
   Interview with Jeanie and Bill Wylie-Kellermann 17

1995
Reading the Building, Seeing the Powers 24

1996
Readers Before Profits 26

1998
To the Hoop Dance: A Grieving Rite 31

2002
Station: A Slot Machine Economy—MGM/Tiger Stadium 38

2004
A Jazz Opera on Detroit Pastor-Organizer 40

2005
Station: Energy Policy, Auto, and War 43

2006
Station: Commodification of Water 45

2007
Station: Detroit River—Undocumented Workers 47

2009
Resurrection City: How Detroit Comes Alive in the New Depression 49
Reading Rivera: Remembering from Post-Industrial Detroit 56

2010
Station: Chase Bank—The Financial Industry 66

2011
Station: Official Violence and Restorative Justice 68

2012
Station: Trayvon Martin and Young Black Males 70
Place-Based Communities of Faith:
   Questions Toward the Beloved Neighborhood 72

EXPULSION SUITE

2013
We Shall Not Be Moved: Words Won't Make it Happen 80
Statements of the Accused: No Consent. Go on Record.
   Come into Exile. 86

2014
Detroit: Is Your City Next? 89
FOR IMMEDIATE RELEASE: Jones Day is Not Detroit 96

Station: New Introductory—Where you put your body 98
Station: Banks and Bankruptcy 100
Poem: A Wager of Love 102
Her Name Was Charity: The Detroit Water Struggle 105
Water Letter: Religious Leaders and Allies 110
Sixty Years Later. In Detroit the End of Brown:
   Separate and Unequal 112

2015
Gentrification and Race: Can We Have a Real Conversation? 120
Poem: For Grace Boggs, at one hundred 134
A Cemetery for Buried Streams 136
From *Wahnabeezee* to PenskeLand:
   The Desecration of Detroit's Belle Isle 139

2016
The Jury is Still Out: The Last Vestige of Democracy 153

Bibliography 157
Subject Index 159

Acknowledgements

Movements and communities are nourished by gratitude. In their way, books too, I suppose. Making thank-you lists should be counted a spiritual practice. Publishing them is a riskier business because omissions are inevitable and mine could never be complete.

Hence and nevertheless this chronicle of big love and prayerful thanks to . . .

Denise Griebler, for suffering and honoring my Detroit place-based vocation, even at the expense of her own, in our common calling of marriage and ministry—for love and care and constant encouragement;

Jeanie Wylie, for being all over these pages and making my heart ache with gratitude;

Charity Hicks, wager of love, to whom they are dedicated;

Tom Lumpkin, Marianne Arbogast, of the Detroit Catholic Worker, and the Detroit Peace Community—nearly four decades of stations, vigils, soup ladling, sacraments, and action;

Monica Lewis-Patrick, Debra Taylor, Marian Kramer, Maureen Taylor, JoAnn Watson, Lila Cabil, Linda Campbell, Piper Carter, Tawana Petty, Alice Jennings, Kim Redigan, Rhonda Anderson, Tangela Harris, Sandra Simmons, Tawana Simpson, Helen Moore, among the movement mothers who teach me and make justice in this town;

Gloria House, also among them, not just for her kind and careful foreword, and the sage advice I probably should have taken, but for being together in so much common work;

Another, Elena Herrada, chronic blogger, co-conspirator, and erstwhile codefendant who has this past decade shaped and sharpened my Detroit political vision as much as any other person;

Kehben Grier and Patrick Perry and the BeeHive Design Collective for this gorgeous cover—the art of politics and the politics of art;

Michelle Martinez and the Swimming in the Detroit River environmental justice writing group who provoked some of these pieces;

Daughters Lydia and Lucy, for being Detroiters on the street and in conscience, reviving *On the Edge* so as to be my editor for some of these and more;

Mike Zelinsky, a bright and joyous light in the Detroit Newspaper Strike, Readers United, the ten direct action groups they organized, the clergy and politicians who stood behind us when we were called before the NRLB, the Strike to Win Caucus, the staff of the *Detroit Sunday Journal*, and of course the strikers themselves.

Civil disobedients resisting corporate fascism and water shutoffs: Herb Sanders, Catherine Phillips, Denise Griebler, Antonio Cosme, Will Copeland, Terry Kelly, Elena Herrada, Luke Mattson, Charity Hicks, Valerie Jean, Daniel Eggert, Phil Dage, Nicole Conway, Mary Ellen Howard, Agnes Hitchcock and, of course, the Homrich 9—Marian Kramer, Baxter Jones, Joan Smith, Jim Perkinson, Hans Barbe, David Olson, Marianne McGuire, Kim Redigan;

Lawyers Jerry Goldberg, Vanessa Fluker, Ralph Simpson, Alice Jennings, Tom Blakely, Cynthia Heenan, Buck Davis, Herb Sanders, Mark Francher, John Royal, Julie Hurwitz, Nick Klaus, Bill Goodman, Deborah Choly, and all the National Lawyers Guild attorneys, for defending us all in the legal arena;

Newly formed and quickly growing, Detroit Independent Freedom School Movement;

Tom Stephens, Shea Howell, Julia Cuneo, Kim Hinter, Gloria House, Michael Doan, Ami Harbin, Tawanna Petty, Fred Vitale, Emily Katil, and the others of Detroiters Resisting Emergency Management for thinking, writing, organizing;

Nelson and Joyce Johnson of Greensboro, for being here when the struggle turned and naming that moment;

Bryce Detroit, Will Copeland, and Lydia Wylie-Kellermann, of Detroit Spirit and Roots for the discernment of spirited organizing and for schooling Word and World in hip hop and indigenous spirituality;

Jimmy Boggs for moving to Detroit and Grace Lee Boggs for living nearly to 100 and leaving nothing unreimagined; and to their {r}evolutionary progeny who created a new community from below;

St. Peter's Episcopal for doing and for being a beloved community and base from which to preach and prophesy, teach and write, act and be;

Lily Mendoza and Jim Perkinson for reading many of these pieces in our living room writers group and for other readers past—Tana Moore, Joel Nigg, Elena Herrada, Tommy and Lindsay Airey, Lydia and Jeanie Wylie-Kellermann, and of course, Denise Griebler;

William Stringfellow, Walter Wink, and Daniel Berrigan, all of blessed memory, for still mentoring me in such things this side of the vale;

Kate Levy (a wonder among us), Piper Carter, Jean Vortcamp, Leona Macalvane, Stephen Boyle, Daymon Hartley, Jose Cuello, Rebecca Cook, Jim West, David Turnley, Jean Vortcamp, Stephanie Mae, Michell Martinez, Mary and Lisa Luvanos, Nora Chapas Mendoza, William Luca and Antonio Cosme, visual visionaries capturing Detroit movement in stills, image, video;

Diego Rivera for being so shrewd and brilliant an artist in giving us the Detroit Industrial Murals.

Aneb Kotsile, Tawana Petty, Michael Lauchlan, Aurora Harris, M. L. Libler, Ron Allen, Jim Perkinson, Will See, Bryce Detroit, Invincible, Lolita Hernandez, The Raiz Up, Sacramento Knox, Christie Beeber, Bill Boyer, the Layabouts, Julie Beutel, Ange Smith, Bill Meyer, Straight Ahead, Harold McKinney, Marcus Belgrave (no, don't start down the endless jazz line),

Detroit poets and musicians whose words and tunes run beneath these essays like a stream:

Whitaker School of Theology, Seminary Consortium for Urban Pastoral Education in Chicago (now since gutted, looted, and left for dead), Marygrove College, Ecumenical Theological Seminary, New Brunswick Seminary, all of whom allowed the teaching of Urban Principalities and the Angel of Detroit;

Norm Thomas, JoAnn Watson, Charles Williams I & II, Maurice Rudd, David Bullock, Abdula ElAmin, Alana Albert, Dawud Walid, Edwin Rowe, Jill Zundell, Tom Lumpkin, Matthew Bode, Lindsay Anderson, Leah McCulloch, Denise Griebler, Areeta Bridgemohan, Gary Bennett, Baye Landy, clergy partners too few and too far between who will stand up to this mess;

Terry Kelly and staff of *The Michigan Citizen*, most progressive paper out there and the most reliable source on Emergency Management and movement news, now gone to history and the archives with the ache of loss, and to other journalists looking the city in the eye and never flinching, Eric Campbell, Zenobia Jeffries, Curt Guyette, Shea Howell, Kim Hunter, Jeanie Wylie, Frank Joyce, Nkenge Zola, the Fifth Estate, David Watson, Peter Werbe, *Motor City Muckraker*, and often as not the *Metro Times*.

Wipf and Stock Publishers, for navigating the waters of a sea change in publishing—and for having Stringfellow, Catholic Worker and Resistance "shelves."

And for Movement forums and publications who have earlier carried the content of this book . . .

Sojourners Magazine

"Discerning the Angel of Detroit: The Spirits and Powers at Work in One City," October 1989

"Readers Before Profits," January/February 1996

"Resurrection City: How Detroit Comes Alive in the New Depression," May 2009

Reprinted with permission from Sojourners, (800) 714-7474, www.sojo.net

Geez Magazine

"Water Witness," Spring 2016

The Record—The Episcopal Diocese of Michigan
"Reading Rivera: Resurrection and Remembering in Post-Industrial Detroit," December 2009

Temple University Press from *Detroit Lives*, Robert H. Mast, ed. (1994) for "Jeanie and Bill Wylie-Kellermann"

Detroit MetroTimes
"In Courts Divine: My Life in the Game," April 1–7 2009

On the Edge—The Detroit Catholic Worker
"A Jazz Opera on Detroit Pastor-Organizer" Fall 2004
"Sixty Years Later. In Detroit the End of Brown: Separate and Unequal" Winter 2014
"Gentrification and Race: Can We Have a Real Conversation?" Spring 2015
"A Cemetery for Buried Streams" Summer 2015

Boggs Center for Community Leadership
Detroit Reader, 2012–
"Place-based Communities of Faith: Questions Toward the Beloved Neighborhood"

Secret Society of Twisted Story Tellers, March 21, 2014—Charles Wright Museum of African American History, Detroit "We Shall Not be Moved: Words Won't Make it Happen"

The Catholic Worker NYC
"Detroit: Is Your City Next?" January–February 2014
"Her Name Was Charity: The Detroit Water Struggle," October–November 2014

Critical Moment
Poem for Charity Hicks—"The greatest of these: wage Love," Fall 2014

Radical Discipleship
Poem: For Grace Boggs, at one hundred

https://radicaldiscipleship.net/

Detroiters Resisting Emergency Management www.d-rem.org
"From Wahnabeezee to PenskeLand: The Desecration of Detroit's Belle Isle"
"Press Release, January 4, 2014: Jones Day is not the City of Detroit"

Cover Story

Water-colored and line-drawn by members of the BeeHive Design Collective, that pheasant on the cover is more deeply Detroit than one might imagine. Since white flight and deindustrialization have rendered 40 percent of the city, thirty square miles, feral grasslands—blocks and tracts and plots of it—I have more than once been surprised to suddenly flush up a pheasant from the foliage. They are common to spot, strutting their distinctive feathers. In the 80's, and perhaps still, the Department of Natural Resources used to transplant Detroit pheasants to areas of the state they sought to re-inhabit. Presumably, the premise went, if they could make it here on the street, they could make it anywhere.

The artists draw this bird almost mythic, rising up Phoenix-like from the city, evoking Detroit's historic motto "We hope for better things, it will rise from the ashes," following the big fire. Could the image be a stand-in for the very Angel of Detroit? It surely hints at the threat of resurrection—and for that my heart is most glad.

I am so grateful to have work of the collective grace this cover. The BeeHive is a group of movement illustrators, political translators, and metaphor makers. Founded in the spring of 2000 (think battle of Seattle) and based in Machias, Maine with collaborators scattered over the hemisphere, they are notorious for their large-scale narrative posters, graphic political novels on a single sheet, layered with history and analysis. Historically, their artistic kin would be Hieronymus Bosch or Pieter Breugel. I have used their work in teaching seminarians about the principalities and powers of this world system.

One of their large-scale projects tells the story of the coal industry's true cost—from fallen ancient ferns to mountain top removal, global warming, and resistance. It was released in Detroit at the 2010 US Social Forum. Another, in two panels, maps the institutions of neoliberalism: the World

Bank, the International Monetary Fund, The North American Free Trade Agreement crisscrossing the hemisphere in ships—discovery, slaving, resource extraction, tourist boats, all pirates riding the winds of privatization, deregulation, and austerity. But just below, underneath and behind, is an intricately drawn bio-community of Meso-American resistance—which one may study, imagining and furthering its ways.

No wonder for good and sequential reason they have now come to Detroit and are listening for the story of struggle here. We too face structural adjustment, privatized resource extraction. I'm glad to be part of the conversation they have provoked and convened. In fact, much of my own story and much of the history recounted in this book, I have shared with them. By turns, I have learned from their gifts and work (the picture, it seems, is partly in the process).

It is no surprise that with others we share a common love for the Anishinaabe name for this place, *Wawiatonong*, translated for us as "where the water goes aound." Many Detroiters will recognize the name and the image as a teaser poster for their planned graphic narrative. Here, in two houses they tell the assault of disinvestment. Imagine, as they did, a running street of buildings and vehicles that stitches together a history of Detroit. Though this pheasant image may not appear in their final illustration I am grateful the drawing has a life as the cover of this book. My heart gives thanks for the BeeHive Collective. May the Spirit bless their work.

Foreword

Gloria House

Where the Water Goes Around is a journey tracing the relationship between place, personal identity, and accountability to community. Specifically, the book reflects Bill Wylie-Kellermann's love of Detroit, and charts his committed involvement in the political struggles that have shaped the city's recent history. He recounts a broad range of experiences, effectively grounding the reader in the world where he is rooted: the remembered excursions of his childhood and those with his own children; the moment in 1967 when as a teenager he sees the smoke from the fires of rebellion, and knows which side he's on; his sense of intimate connection with the treasured nineteenth- century island park, Belle Isle; the claiming of direct action as a means by which he will incarnate the Christian teachings; and his consciousness that beneath the Motor City sidewalks and freeways run the ancient waterways and pathways of indigenous sovereignty and reverence for the land.

There are provocative musings that lead us to perceive urban life from unfamiliar perspectives, like the essay on the city as spiritual power. There are recurring references to the historic imprint of Detroit's working class. There are compelling stories—of Lewis Bradford, a radical pastor among factory workers, of Diego Rivera, the great Mexican muralist, whose profoundly humanist philosophy continues to teach from the walls of the Detroit Institute of Arts; and of Charity Hicks, Detroit's brilliant African American environmentalist whose tragic death followed closely after her brave resistance to water shutoffs in her neighborhood. And of great informational and practical value to cultural workers and political organizers, there are detailed reports on the exploitative policies that have led to the city's present-day corporate reclamation and dispossession of the people of color. If one wants to understand what has become of Detroit in the last two decades—the impact of emergency management, the illegal imposition of bankruptcy—here are the necessary commentaries.

The devastation that has been wrought upon the actual landscape of the city and the quality of life citizens once enjoyed is hard for outsiders to fathom. The takeover of the city by an emergency manager working to serve corporate interests and the designs of a Republican governor has been so ruthless as to be unimaginable for those living outside the wreckage. When Detroiters tell our friends around the county that thousands of families are living without running water in their homes because of the massive water shutoffs ordered by the Detroit Water and Sewerage Department; when we point out that there is no longer a public health department; when we bemoan the total dismantlement of our public school system to make way for privatized, corporate-managed charters, the response is often a dazed silence. Wylie-Kellermann's essays document the outrageously lawless tactics and strategies that have brought this havoc, the ways in which corporations and foundations have undermined and circumvented the democratic processes of city government. Such practices have ensured that every African American city in Michigan is no longer governed by its elected officials, but by appointed emergency managers. These essays help us grasp the unprecedented, inhumane scale of social destabilization that has been fostered by policies of "austerity" in a major American city. This is essential reading.

As pastor of the historic St. Peter's Church, located in a neighborhood now slated for "redevelopment," and the preferred "R and R" neighborhood for many of the city's poor and homeless, Wylie-Kellermann has sought to make the essence of the Christian gospel come alive for those suffering hardships. To that end, his congregation collaborates with a number of organizations to provide a soup kitchen, to make water available, and to extend other survival services. Another aspect of this ministry is the exciting "liturgy of place" that Wylie-Kellermann and a small group of like-minded community activists are forging. They borrow the symbolism of the Christian stations of the cross, but take their observances *outside* the church sanctuary. In walking meditations, they inscribe the intention of community within a circumference of city blocks, anointing sites with song, prayer, and Scripture. This is a very useful model for those seeking to attune spirituality and social justice advocacy.

We follow Wylie-Kellermann from these evolving rituals of his church community into multiple other arenas of political engagement—to meetings of the Detroit City Council, study groups, cultural projects, and into direct actions to resist injustices of many kinds, from a kneel-in to protest approval of an emergency manager contract, to an early morning blocking of the trucks of contracted workers scheduled to carry out water shutoffs. For Wylie-Kellermann, nonviolent direct action is a way to live the Christian principle of standing with "the least of these."

Closing *Where the Water Goes Around*, we are thankful for these disclosures of a life of multilayered political consciousness and engagement. Through Wylie-Kellermann's actions and reflections, we understand more clearly the oppressive forces we are up against. Moreover, we affirm and celebrate the personal, spiritual, and political resources that we have at our disposal for fashioning creative, new strategies of resistance.

Detroit
October 14, 2015

Introduction

I am a native-born Detroiter, a white male in a black majority city—actually one of the few remaining major cities in the nation with an African American majority. For years that's given me great joy. I am a pastor, in an educated and privileged profession, but I try to be so as an ally in the prophetic tradition. When I think about my calling, my vocation as a pastor and even as a human being, I cannot not envision Detroit. I believe I actually have a place-based vocation.

One of the essays in this book concerns parishes, "place-based churches," and therein I mention the vows of stability taken by many monastic orders, a commitment to sit tight, stay in place, looking for the presence of God here and here and here again.

Mine is like that. When I contemplated the vocation of marriage I had to set it beside my commitment to Detroit, and sort that out from the patriarchal if not patrilocal presumptions of my culture. It was just a given, even if a pushy one, to say, "This is my beloved ground and I know I'm not going nowhere."

When I graduated from Cooley High School in 1967, my senior year term paper, where one learned in those days to do research using note cards, was on Gandhi, Martin Luther King, and civil disobedience. I stumbled upon it in my attic several years ago. Given my history of action, court, and jail time since, it was a sweet and ironic discovery. I know it colored how I read certain events the following summer.

In June of 1967, I found myself in northwest Detroit when the fires of the Great Rebellion got lit. I have a memory of standing in the middle of Grand River Avenue (can that literally be?) and looking toward downtown to see the smoke rising. The image and its meaning are etched in my consciousness like an icon. My vocation—pastoral, personal, locational—passes through that moment and vision. My feet found their roots on the spot. Though I've gone elsewhere to study or start projects, I've been called home. I've been here continuously going on four decades now.

It was a lovely shock to realize I'd written a book on Detroit. Generally what I write is short and tied to a particular moment of social struggle. It is theology and politics—in the service of movement. These past two years have been brutally intense for the city, and I produced a clutch of essays that seemed to have a natural coherence—on emergency management, the dismantling of public education, the Detroit water struggle, gentrification, and the desecration of Belle Isle—the city's island park. Because each as a lens names the times so clearly I began to think I ought to pull them together in a pamphlet of sorts. They appear at the conclusion of the book, grouped as the Expulsion Suite, and since they are most current, some readers may want jump straight there to begin, then backtrack. When I set to editing the suite, I suddenly realized I'd been putting these things out for thirty-five years and I'd actually written a book. One may be right on time for Detroit's current struggle and changes.

Gustavo Cabrera, of SIPAZ in Mexico, says "There are some places where you can take the temperature of the world. Chiapas is one of them." He's right. And another one is Detroit.

Over the decades Detroit has been abandoned by white folks, by industries (auto chief among them), by capital investment, all the elements of a tax base. And yet Detroit is a border city, with an international crossing, set to double its commercial traffic. It has a future as an international port. As the climate crisis looms, it sits on the banks of 20 percent of the world's fresh water. Two-fifths of the city is "vacant" land eyed for development. The corporations which fled it, now want it back.

So our city is a hot topic these days. In national and even global media, you can find stuff on all the narratives current: the proving ground for municipal bankruptcy; the blank slate awaiting the hand of culturally creative saviors; the failed black city coming back (to white); the financial disaster crying opportunity; the city saved by emergency management, a new white mayor, and the nerd governor who (until the Flint water crisis) some thought should run for president. Now sort through all of these reading for race, class, and white presumption.

To all those, I pray this book is a counter-narrative. Though told in a white voice it is nonetheless different. It is more difficult to find than the marketed narratives, and so harder to come by. Reading through these essays, I'm made more aware of my own white presumptions. That is a confession and names a process of repentance that I hope is also apparent. But generally these are accounts told from below, from the perspective of movement and community. They sometimes inhabit a geography which the Scriptures and politicos call "exile" and are told against the backdrop of empire. They listen for the suffering cry, what my friend Jim Perkinson calls, "the groan." They tell the struggles that are sparked by that cry. They are a narrative that follows the call we have recently heard from Charity Hicks, to "Wage Love."

Friends of ours in the Watershed Discipleship movement (and this surely is a watershed moment for the city) frequently say, "You can't change a place you don't love. And you can't love a place you don't know."

In the late seventies I taught a course for Episcopalians on "Discerning the Angel of Detroit." Looking back on it now, I think of it as a course about knowing and loving this city. Predicated on the letters to the seven churches at the beginning of the book of Revelation, it sought to get at the genius or the spirit of the city. Detroit actually has a sculpture at the Coleman A. Young Municipal Building called the Spirit of Detroit, so in public discourse it seemed we were halfway there. The course involved a reading of city history, an analysis of structure and culture, and finally a poetic discernment exercise of writing a letter to the heart of the city.

Such a letter is one way of getting at the spirit/angel, but also of naming the moment. Discerning the times is a constant task of church and movement. In Greek there are two words for time—*chronos,* as in chronometer or chronic, is clock time. The other word, the one used constantly in the second testament, is *kairos* and means time more as a ripening or fulfillment. It's been given theological and political resonance by its use in various international Kairos Documents because each of them names an urgent moment of crisis and opportunity where God is breaking into history. The Gospels read Jesus' march into Jerusalem as the *kairos* of its visitation (Luke 19:44). In some sense each of the essays in this book are attempts to discern the times of Detroit at any given moment.

Grace Lee Boggs took the course. At this writing she has just joined the ancestors at 100. She was a creative participant in pretty much every social movement of the last seventy years. To see a movement institution (with a PhD in social philosophy from Bryn Mawr) walk into your class is a tad intimidating. I won't say we team-taught the course, but there certainly was more than one voice in the lead. The history and vision she brought certainly shaped what I eventually wrote under that same title. But I am also aware that it was about that time that she and her cohort began speaking of the need to "reimagine, rebuild, and respirit Detroit." The essay that was born out of that course is the first in this book.

In the period when it seemed "no one was in charge," and there was great freedom for Detroiters to build a resurrected post-industrial city from the ground up, *Sojourners* asked me to reprise the angel article. The article, included, overlaps some with a substantial piece on the Detroit Industrial Murals which were painted by Diego Rivera at the Detroit Institute of Arts. The latter is full of my own political theology and a good bit of Detroit history, especially from the thirties. It was prepared for the Detroit US Social Forum of 2010 and published by the thousands in *The Record* of the Episcopal Diocese of Michigan, whose editor was then Herb Gunn. Thanks be. The article led to something of a shtick, doing Rivera tours for friends and visitors and learning more and more from each telling and conversation. The most satisfying thing from that oral and published account is to hear key points become commonplace in other people's descriptions of the mural. I have added endnotes, distinct from the original footnotes, to convey some of the lessons I've learned and elaborated in subsequent tours. Thank you all.

One portion edited out of that piece was a section on "Forgotten," this jazz musical about a Detroit worker-pastor murdered in the Rouge Plant in that same period, the early thirties. I did so mainly because I've included a full review which ran in a number of publications. My wife Jeanie and I met and hosted its author, Steve Jones, as he was researching and writing. Our own story ended up influencing its construction in a simple way.

There is included an interview with Jeanie and me from a book edited by Robert Mast called *Detroit Lives*. The title works no matter how you pronounce it. For Jeanie's part that included material on the 1980 struggle to save the Poletown neighborhood from destruction and clearing for a Cadillac plant; for mine it included biblical theology. Mast was mainly doing interviews with labor left, freedom struggle folks, and we were hard to place in a tidy way. We ended up leading off a section of the book called, "City Life, Scenes and Feelings." In rereading, I'm pleased how well it stands up.

The time we did fully enter into the labor community was during the Detroit Newspaper strike of 1995. We'd fallen in love and married in the context of antinuclear resistance, especially around a cruise missile engine factory in the northern suburbs. The strike was the point where we brought nonviolent direct action to bear heavily on a specifically Detroit struggle. After taking on the Pentagon and the military industrial complex, this seemed to us a winnable local effort. We were slow to realize we were actually up against global corporations with deep, deep pockets that they were willing to use to break the unions. We learned to love a new culture—smoky beer-soaked dinners to fundraise and rally. Except for the smoke and beer, it was a lot like church—something solid and radical at the heart, but timidified and compromised, by race, bureaucracy, and business models. The faithful fought on from below.

Jeanie and I worked closely and incredibly well in the strike. We were effortlessly in sync. Eventually we were called before the National Labor Relations Board fishing for charges, but we came with a roomful of bishops, city council members, and civic leaders who covered out backs politically. Apart from the Angel of Detroit, this one is most theologically specific pieces in framing a story around the biblical notion of the "principalities and powers," generally so crucial to my teaching and writing. If you pay attention here, you'll come to recognize the theological subtext in subsequent chapters. The strike, forced by the company, was a genuine assault on the city and its labor community. And the strike council was in fact way too timid. Only worse since. Michigan is now a right-to-work state. I wrote about the strike and of Readers United in a variety of places. A portion of what's here is part of a book on the death and life of my sweet partner, *Dying Humanly: The Resurrected Life of Jeanie Wylie-Kellermann*.

Perhaps the quirkiest article herein is one on my life in basketball. It was also the publishing coup of my career. I wrote it to honor and grieve one of my early retirements from the game. Less theological (though it could have been), it's full of politics, jail time, and the like. I initially just copied it for hand-to-hand circulation among a cohort of courtmate friends, but then the NCAA basketball finals came to San Antonio, Texas where the owners of the *Detroit MetroTimes* had another weekly rag of culture and politics. They needed something for the cover and my love tome came to their attention. They cleaned out a lot of the Detroit stuff to make it more generic and, lo and behold, I was a cover story for the Final Four weekend. With the stipend I bought a backyard hoop for my daughters, then showing interest. End of story? No. Some years later the Final Four came to Detroit. On a long shot I floated it to the new editor of the *MetroTimes* who liked and wanted it immediately. I needed him to know it had been previously published in the *San Antonio Current*, and he said, "No problem, that's one of ours." So it ran a second time on the cover for the Big Dance, this time in all its detailed Detroit glory. That's the version found here.

In the book, chapters are organized chronologically by year of publication. That means you can see lessons learned and changing patterns of my thought. Substantially filling a gap at one point, but woven throughout, are short meditations from our community's stations of the cross walk each Good Friday. The route and the meditations are always different, reflecting the changing landscape of history and events. In a partnership between my congregation, St. Peter's Episcopal, and the Detroit Catholic Worker, we take each Lent as a time to discern where Christ is being crucified today. Then we divide up responsibilities for writing a one-page meditation. I always write at least one and have included some of those along with a couple of introductory pages from the booklet.

Speaking of crucifixion, be warned that the last sections bear a good bit of passion and pain.

Detroit, like every major black city in the state, has been taken over by a form of corporate fascism, illegitimate and unconstitutional. If this is news to you, you're in for a series of shocks in these chapters. Emergency management itself is one story—all the powers of government and more vested in one person. But the consequences of that for the systematic destruction of public education may take your breath away.

Another subset of the emergency manager resistance has been the Detroit Water Struggle. Each summer for the past two years a private contractor has set about shutting off water to 25,000 homes in the city—anyone two months or $150 behind in payment. The assault figures into the privatization or regionalization of the Detroit Water and Sewage and it is also part of a massive geographic restructuring of the city, largely on behalf of white people. Our church has become a water station for urgent distribution and six of our members have been part of direct actions blocking the shutoff trucks from going out on their deadly errand. The account here revolves around Charity Hicks, an environmental justice activist who resisted her own shutoff and sparked the struggle, nearly in the manner of Rosa Parks. Struck by a hit-and-run driver in New York, she died in the summer of 2014. This book is dedicated to her spirit and memory.

The last essays (emergency management, destruction of public education, the water struggle, gentrification, and the desecration of our island park Belle Isle) are all connected and came in such quick succession. They are the ones I first reconceived as a kind of pamphlet to be published, effectively seeding this book. They are also a sober and heavy conclusion to a story which I would rather end with resurrection.

Actually, resurrection is here, beginning to end, end to beginning. Look for it. In the closing pages resurrection is resistance. It's the refusal to cede death the last word. It's certainly in the rising movement, led notoriously by strong African American women. They teach me over and over. As I write that, I become mindful that I have not adequately told that story in these pages. They are present in the acknowledgments and in the final chapter on the water trial. But Charity stands among them and for them.

This account of Detroit told from where I sit, is unfinished—and that too may be a space for resurrection to inhabit. I send it off with a jury till out. The present times are hard—harder than any I've known here. But things may indeed be turning unbeknownst. The final paragraphs of the Belle Isle essay are a kind of apocalyptic prayer. Who knows if it is already being answered?

1989

Discerning the Angel of Detroit: The Spirits and Powers at Work in One City

SOJOURNERS MAGAZINE, OCTOBER 1989

> THE CITY [in Hebrew] is 'iyr or 'iyr re'em. Now this word has several meanings. It is not only the city, but also the Watching Angel, the Vengeance and the Terror.... We must admit that the city is not just a collection of houses with ramparts, but also a spiritual power. I am not saying it is a being. But like an angel it is a power, and what seems prodigious is that its power is on a spiritual plane. —The Meaning of the City, by Jacques Ellul

In the hot summer of 1988 something happened in Detroit. A well-financed campaign to legalize and develop casino gambling as the panacea for the city's desperate, ongoing economic crisis was rejected overwhelmingly at the polls.

Oh, yes, there was a hard-working, no-budget counter-campaign by neighborhood organizations, and a stiffening in certain city pulpits. But perhaps something more was at work...

One neighborhood activist who served a token appointment on the mayor's blue-ribbon committee studying the issue offered a minority report of solid arguments and reasons, then groped further, to the brink of something more: "I don't know, I'm not sure how to say this. Detroit is a blue-collar town. Its essential character is just a bad fit for casinos, with their big money and glitz. From an image perspective, it just doesn't work."

What if the city of Detroit, its spirit and identity, was an ally, most unacknowledged, in the fight against the casino invasion? That would be a political (and theological) insight worth pursuing.

Recent exegetical work and theological reflection on the principalities and powers suggests a versatile but coherent New Testament cosmology that recognizes the spiritual dimension of institutions and social structures. One which may be verified in our experience.

As the letter to the church in the city of Colossae implies, these structures are simultaneously material and spiritual, seen and unseen, interior and exterior, earthly and heavenly. They are expressed in two poles of reality as it were. "For in [Christ] all things were created, in heaven and on earth, visible and invisible, whether thrones or dominions or principalities or authorities—all things were created through Christ and for Christ" (Col 1:16).

It is an interesting exercise in first-century "social analysis" to apply these political categories to the city of Detroit:

The *throne* is the seat of power; that is, the mayor's office, the council chamber, the Monoogian Mansion where the mayor lives.

Dominion is the realm or territory, even the sphere of influence. Here one thinks first of municipal boundaries, such as Eight Mile Road. But its social and political influence (much diminished these days) in the Tri-County Area or the State Capitol should be counted as well. Dominion consists of those places and ways the city's authority penetrates the lives of its people.

The *principality*, the prince, is the agent-in-role, the ruler-in-office: with respect to the executive, not Coleman Alexander Young, but Mayor Young.

Authorities are the range of sanctions and legitimations by which authority is maintained. A longer list comes to mind, from the cops and courts to rituals like election campaigning, press conferences, ground breakings, and photo opportunities; or symbols like the city charter, the seal, those billboards proclaiming city sponsorship at this or that development site, and the mayor's image hung in front offices everywhere, from city clerk to neighborhood police ministration. You can think of more.

The elements are not exhaustive. Among other things they omit economic seats of power such as the auto companies or bank board rooms or the multinational powers of illegal commerce like the drug cartels that open street level "branch offices," each of which has its own spirituality.

Moreover, the political administration and the city as an entity name two very distinct powers. The City of Detroit (which one may look up in the telephone book and with persistence eventually reach) is not the same in this sense as Detroit the city. It may presume to speak for the city, but the two voices are not one and the same. It may try to claim the rich history or the spirit of the city, but these are not its own to manipulate or dispose of.

THE CITY AS A SPIRITUAL POWER

After the biblical manner of the angels of the nations (portrayed most dramatically in Daniel 10) or the angels of the churches (addressed in the opening chapters of Revelation), I have begun to speak of the "angel of Detroit." The term piques and intrigues. By it I mean what has been called the "actual inner spirituality" of the city. I mean to get at its identity and vocation, its character and personality, its potentiality as well as its fallenness before God.

One of the first to write about the city in this fashion was Jacques Ellul. Because his book *The Meaning of the City* was something of a theological companion to his devastating sociological work *The Technological Society*, but also because Ellul's theology simply goes this way, it is relentlessly pessimistic about the character of the city as a human work and its predatory fallenness as a spiritual power. (One hastens to add that in keeping with his theology, Ellul is also radically hopeful about God's grace, judging the city but adopting it nevertheless as an instrument of grace.)

The idea that the city is at once a human work and a spiritual power is a mystery key to any understanding of the principalities (of which the city may be said, in Ellul's view, to be the very prototype). It is in this regard that Ellul mines the mythic primeval history of Genesis with astonishing results.

Who, do you happen to recall, was the first builder of a city? It was Cain. As a resident of Detroit, whose media monikers notoriously include "Murder City," I find my ears perk up.

Banished to a life of wandering and insecurity, "He built a city and called the name of the city after the name of his son Enoch" (Gen 4:17). By murder Cain has broken his relationship to humanity, to God, and even to the earth (which received Abel's blood and cried out to the Lord). He has destroyed his home and so sets out to build his own security, the city named Enoch, meaning "initiation" or "dedication." Cain's bold pretension is to construct and dedicate his own new world. Violence is the kernel of alienation by which the brave new city is seeded.

And idolatry. Here we think most readily of the tower of Babel. "And they said to one another, 'Come, let us build ourselves a city, and a tower with its top in the heavens, and let us make a name for ourselves'" (Gen 11:4). The tower, says Ellul, is not the center of the narrative; the city and the name are. The one is the means to the other. But name here means not so much reputation and notoriety as becoming independent, making their own name.

It is now widely understood that naming in Israelite culture has a supreme importance. It signifies dominion. It is a token of spiritual power. The city, then, is not a Promethean act reaching up to God. It is the act of making an identity by making a world, an urban environment, a great city. It is the act of excluding God from creation. It is incipient and express idolatry. So Ellul's radical pessimism.

Here we are at the mystery of works become fallen, of demonic powers. Here is the truth of Enoch and Babel and Babylon and Rome and New York and, alas, even Detroit. Insofar as human beings find meaning and justification and identity in the city, they make its angel a fallen angel.

William Stringfellow used to say that the vocation of the principalities was to praise God and serve human life. I like the image of Detroit singing in the courts of God, not to mention serving its own inhabitants. I know, however, that it suffers blindness, confusion, inflation, and distortion in the fall.

As Jesus approached Jerusalem, he paused to address it. "Would that even today you knew the things that make for peace." (Jerusalem's name means "foundation of peace," though it suffered a deep confusion and blindness.) "But now they are hid from your eyes. For the days shall come upon you, when your enemies will cast up a bank about you and surround you, and hem you in on every side, and dash you to the ground, you and your children within you, and they will not leave one stone upon another in you; because you did not know the *kairos* of your visitation" (Luke 19:42-44).

Walter Wink, who has done so much good work in recent years on the powers, points out that each of the pronouns in this passage is singular. Jesus addresses the city as an entity: you. Dare we say he has discerned the angel of Jerusalem and spoken to it? First he names and addresses it, claiming the dominion of the Word of God, then he enters its symbolic center with the strong action at the temple.

Several things strike as noteworthy clues within. One, if we accept the synoptic portrayal of events where this is his first glimpse, Jesus discerns the angel of Jerusalem in Galilee! Perhaps this should not be so surprising. The city's dominion, its sphere of influence spiritual and political and economic, dominated the region. To abide with the poor of Galilee was to feel the weight of the temple City, to know its true character, because they were beholden to its aristocracy, its obligations, its interests.

In Galilee Jesus felt its influence, as evidenced by his temptations and again later through its intimidations. "O Jerusalem, Jerusalem, killing the prophets and stoning those who are sent to you! How often would I have gathered your children together as a hen gathers her brood under her wings, and you would not! Behold, your house is forsaken" (Luke 13:34-35).

There is love here. It is the agonized love that causes Jesus to break down in tears, even as he approaches the city to confront and rebuke its power. By such accounts, Jesus loves Jerusalem, longs for it to praise God and serve human life. I don't know if that is prerequisite to discernment, but he does yearn that it should recognize this *kairos*, this opportunity wherein it might repent and recover its calling before God.

All right, emboldened by the Lord, I admit it: I love Detroit. I love that it's a movement town. The home of the sit-down strike. Rich in a history of struggle. Count the left groups and factions that have their official headquarters at this prodigious address. Martin Luther King Jr. tried out both his "I Have a Dream" speech and the Vietnam renunciation in Detroit first. They flew.

I love the black majority and even revel in the scandal that it is to the American norm. The '67 rebellion burns in my high school consciousness like a revelatory moment, a personal and political turning point. Not that de facto segregation doesn't carve up neighborhoods (and churches), but I delight in the wealth of street culture.

There's so much of the South in Detroit's black, and white, community—family and extended kinship and hospitality and old-fashioned morality. Waves were drawn north by the auto companies, much like the Europeans before who still cluster by culture in neighborhoods. I love the Hispanic barrio on the southwest side where we live, and the fact that Detroit has the largest Arab population this side of the Middle East.

I love the legacy of Motown soul, the gospel music, and the Detroit jazz within it. I love Tiger Stadium and confess my loyalty to certain of the city's athletic teams.

I love the river. The straits, from which the French name, *de troit*, is our link with the Great Lakes ecosystem. I love Belle Isle, the huge island park that is the chief recreational resource of the city's poor. There mix the smells of river water and barbecue.

I love the city. And I dread it, too. And sometimes I weep. So, is that prerequisite to discerning the angel of Detroit? Maybe.

In spring 1989 a handful of activists and church people who are engaged in ministry or social struggle in Detroit met for six weeks with this precise project in mind. They committed themselves to bringing the city as an entity into their established spiritual disciplines. To intercede for the city in prayer. To hold it in heart during Scripture study. To attend to its spirit in journal keeping.

The immediate concrete project was to write something in the voice of the city or to address the Word to Detroit in this historical moment, much like the Revelation 2 letters, "To the angel of Detroit write this . . . ." (The latter may seem at first blush pretentious, but no more bold really than a preacher taking the pulpit week after week to speak the Word to a congregation.)

A first question we asked one another concerned geography. Implicitly a question about social location (as Jesus with the Galilean peasantry), it is also a matter of physical place and a stimulus to imagination. John had his Patmos for divining the angel of Rome. Where would we stand to listen for the voice of the city?

By the river at Belle Isle? Above one of the freeway canyons that riddle the city? At Solidarity House, union headquarters? At an empty lot in a devastated neighborhood such as the Cass Corridor? Surrounded by the famous Diego Rivera mural depicting with care and irony industrial Detroit? In Elmwood Cemetery, which retains one of the few plots of original pre-urban terrain?

A few years earlier, by virtue of my part in a neighborhood organization, I had represented the community on a development coalition composed elsewise of institutional and corporate types. Their vision and agenda was different from ours. Still, if we met in the neighborhood the reality of food lines and housing needs, the lives of people, were never completely out of sight and mind. But when they took to meeting in a conference room in the heady heights of the Renaissance Center, a downtown megastructure, our community faded literally into the distance and a different spirit presided.

Discerning the Angel of Detroit: The Spirits and Powers at Work in One City

Outside the City-County Building is a large sculpture called The Spirit of Detroit. Its image is reproduced on city letterheads, documents, and building project signs. More than the city seal, it is the official symbol of Detroit. For that reason the spirit has some currency in political discourse. It is claimed and abused and struggled over.

Sometimes dubbed the "green giant," the sculpture was completed in the 50's by an artist known for war memorials and works on a grand scale, such as the world's largest crucifix in the woods of northern Michigan. Inspired by 2 Corinthians 3:17 that "where the Spirit of the Lord is there is liberty," he set to work. A large figure of humanity, quite male and Scandinavian, holds a golden sphere of the deity in his left hand; and in his right hand, toward which he looks, a nuclear family lifts its arms to heaven.

A museum curator whom I asked about the sculpture thought the divine sphere signified "science and the industrial genius of the auto companies." (There is an annual car show called the Spirit of Detroit.) A city government publication avers, "For many it symbolizes the city's new spirit of renaissance and rebuilding." The City Council confers Spirit of Detroit awards on prominent and worthy citizens. But a group of community organizations fighting for neighborhood priorities over downtown development in the city budget calls itself the Save Our Spirit Coalition.

The sculpture itself marks out a kind of public political space. It is the common site of demonstrations against city administration policies. I once saw a coven of witches gather there to invoke Hecate and curse the world's largest trash incinerator being built within city limits.

Most intriguing is a weekly vigil of the Anti-Handgun Association. At the foot of the sculpture they read aloud a small booklet of facts and the stories of victims. It is a kind of meditation, a liturgy really. Included is a modified verse of the black spiritual: "Were you there when each day a child was shot?" But the refrain at the close of each small section is "Spirit of Detroit, save our youth!" I believe the angel of Detroit is being named and addressed in this little event.

On the other hand, as part of a 1988 ad campaign, a gigantic fez cap (you know, with tassels, like the Shriners wear) was set upon the statue's head to coincide with the appearance of billboards bearing a similar image and announcing that "Conventions are the Spirit of Detroit." Which is to say again that the spirit of the city is a matter of dispute. It is subject to diverse claims, humiliations, and manipulations.

That dispute and the "conventions-as-the-spirit" claim call to mind that Detroit, like so many other cities (or like the nation for that matter, or even the global economy), is a tale of two cities. One is the living city composed of neighborhoods where poor and working people reside, almost entirely in single-family homes. (Until the late 60's, Detroit was the largest homeowning city north of the Mason-Dixon Line.) The other is the new downtown of government-subsidized megastructures: arenas, the convention center, hotels, commercial space, luxury high-rises, and office buildings, all connected by an elevated railway going in circles. Conventioneers and executives never need set foot on the streets of the city.

It is on those megastructures that the administration is banking and betting. Mortgaging the Block Grant budget, funneling grants to large-scale private development, and hustling tax abatements is the official order of the day.

A five-tower skyscraper, this weird urban stalagmite is the emblem, anchor, and centerpiece of the scheme. Spearheaded by auto money, it was built in the wake of the '67 insurrection. Intended to signify a rising from the ashes, a mock resurrection, it was called the Renaissance Center and intended to make a name for Detroit: Renaissance City.

The influence of the insurrection is in its bones. It has an imposing and inaccessible structure, literally defensible. Ringed as it is with a concrete embankment, one readily imagines the location of gun turrets.

I used to think of drafting a theological leaflet summarizing Ellul's Babel reflections and distributing it within. But the only time I ever attempted to leaflet there, we were swarmed by plainclothes private security bearing walkie-talkies and summoning the city cops, who arrived in a flash. (The marketplace at the Renaissance Center as elsewhere is no longer public. It is privately owned. The streets may belong to the people, but the streets are disappearing.)

The RenCen marketplace is a failure, by and large. Its three-story shopping mall with an endless series of circular passages is a nightmare to navigate, the reputed "easiest place to get lost in Detroit." It signifies the failed attempt to move the suburbs downtown, to reverse the drain that has been going on since the first shopping mall in the world, Northland, was built in Detroit—or, more precisely, just outside of it.

Detroit photographers with an eye for the human or the ironic never tire of juxtaposing a glass-strewn lot or the burned shell of a building with the shining towers of the RenCen. The view of one city from the other.

In the decaying neighborhoods, there is a phenomenon that is also a metaphor: brick thievery. An unlicensed dump truck jostles and pulls at the walls of abandoned apartment buildings until the facade collapses. The driver, a maverick subcontractor himself, pays street people day-labor wages to clean and load the bricks into his truck. Neighbors, slow on the uptake, imagine the city has sponsored the demolition. (Indeed 150,000 Detroit homes—nearly half the total—have been burned or bulldozed in recent years. And by current count there are more than 15,000 abandoned buildings in the city.)

Come evening the truck is gone and the frame shell of the building, more exposed and unsafe than ever, remains standing in a pile of rubble. The bricks go for top dollar in the suburbs, where patios, I suppose, get that aged urban character.

Like the suburban boom still going on, downtown development by and large sucks the life, including city budget priorities, out of the neighborhoods. The new office towers drain the business from the older addresses, leaving empty aging tombs on the marginal skyline.

The most notorious and blatant example of such megadevelopment was the 1980 condemnation and destruction of an entire integrated, ethnic neighborhood of 1,200 homes to build a highly automated Cadillac plant. (Two older General Motors plants, including one just blocks from my house, closed simultaneously for a substantial net loss in jobs.) In the Poletown neighborhood, arson aided and abetted the project by driving out the resisting residents and making demolition easier.

The Poletown project marked a turning point in recent Detroit history. A friend of mine calls it "the official sanction to devastation."

And it is also the emblem of Detroit's bondage to the auto industry, to principalities and powers that have fed on the city, its human population, and now have grown larger in scale and scope than the city itself. They move capital, exporting jobs south, or south of the border. By that freedom and threat, they blackmail the city for tax abatements and land. No longer, Do you want General Motors, one of the world's largest corporations, in Detroit? But, Do you want Detroit in General Motors?

Growing up here I shared the fascination with the motorcar. My wife still marvels at my unsuppressed enthusiasm for the useless skill of distinguishing a '55 Chevrolet from a '56. The automobile is deeply entangled not merely with the economy, but with the collective psyche of Motor City. Detroit is a ruined shrine to that version of American consumer idolatry.

At one session of our "Discerning the Angel" group, we tried to bring our own unconscious resources, our right brains, as it is said, into the process by forming an image of Detroit's angel in clay. I found myself shaping up a figure crying out in the grip of a gigantic hand.

Was that hand the power of the multinational auto companies? I think perhaps it was. Though it might in equal portion have been the grip of the cocaine powers.

Not many years ago, one citywide drug-dealing organization, Young Boys, Inc., did $400 million of business annually. Today, crack cocaine sales top a billion dollars a year. The market includes a broad range of users, from the auto worker pulling down $35,000 and spending half of it on crack, to members of the permanent underclass being paid, in effect, in crack "rocks" for the goods they've stolen from their neighbors' homes. The average user has a $250 a week habit.

Crack houses vary, too. On one end is the social crack house, like the "blind pig" of Prohibition days with its "tavern culture," diverse and illicit services, ersatz community, and personal interaction. On the other end is the fortified abandoned building where sales are made through a slot in the door. Some set-ups, as suggested, are fencing operations that exchange cocaine for stolen merchandise.

All of them are arsenals full of weapons. And not just handguns. (In Detroit there are already two of these for every man, woman, and child.) Semi-automatics and Uzis are rife. Enforcers patrol the streets in four-wheel-drive jeeps with tinted glass. Same vehicles and weapons and methods as the Salvadoran death squads, say.

Earlier this year, in a neighborhood on the northwest side, a wave of crack houses invaded. Now with such invasions comes a simultaneous arrival: a palpable spirit of fear and intimidation. You can almost taste the acrid smell, a shadow of death settling in.

Against the houses and their spirit, residents made repeated police calls but without response. Finally one day the cops made a bust, a buyer coming out. Across the street, an older black woman who had made the call raised her arms and rejoiced, "Thank you, Jesus! Thank you!" Some would say she was unduly and indiscreetly bold.

The next morning an ambulance arrived at her home, summoned by a 911 call. A shooting had been reported. She was dumbfounded; they had been misinformed. She didn't know who had called.

On the following day arrived the "dead wagon," as she calls it, from the nearby funeral home. They had been called to pick up the body.

Now these are death threats in the concrete, and sophisticated ones at that, but the older woman was having none of it. She consulted her friend, another senior citizen veteran of the civil rights movement (with which the city is filled) and together they convened a meeting at her church on Rosa Parks Boulevard. "My dreams," one of them later reported, "overtook my fears."

On Friday night next, they met in a storefront, were led in prayer by their Baptist pastor, and there began a slow procession through the community, pausing in front of the known crack houses and singing, "We Shall Overcome." Every third Friday they do it again. And it's catching on in other neighborhoods.

This is an exorcism, dear friends. It is a discernment of the spirit of death and a public rebuke. A refusal of its claim. This is a public liturgy of freedom, for person and community. On a scale at once modest and bold, it is an attempt to set at liberty the neighborhood, indeed the city of Detroit, its angel. Most of us in the angel discernment group have joined them on one occasion or another.

Discernment of spirits. Among the so-called charismatic gifts, it is the political sleeper. But how to go about it, this odd and intuitive grace? In our little group, we did Bible study of Luke, Colossians, Daniel, Cain, and Babel. We heard a poet read glimpses of his loving urban realism. We watched a film and played with clay. We talked and talked about what we love and hate about Detroit and how it is at a historical turning point. But in the end we listened. We found the time, chose geography (I did go to Belle Isle), and sat to listen and write. The most wonderful things came forth.

At our last group session, we read our work to one another. It was nothing less than a liturgical event. More than once we came to tears.

One of these "prophecies" (let's call them that) was a plaintive plea in the city's voice, "Here I am, listen to me now." Weak but not beaten, tired but not driven out. A voice in cries and whispers from the river, the alleys, the boarded homes and closed shops, and the places of power. A voice driven underground, but yearning to be called out and heeded.

Another was confessional and repentant, naming its pulsing heart in neighborhood life, but confessing the temptations of big-ticket development.

One, in the loving voice of the Lord God, chastised the angel for succumbing to the seductions and illusions of material affluence, the appetites that willingly tolerate injustice for the continuing paycheck. And for failing to take on the struggle against the multinational corporations that left Detroit, a losing struggle but one which, if articulated, could have helped save the soul of the city's people.

Yet another was a meditation focused on the sculpture, "A Message to the Spirit of Detroit from the One who was dead but now lives." It called the spirit to attend to its family, especially the children and youth, by turning its eyes to the divine energy that alone can renew.

There were more. I do none of them justice. Were they definitive? No. Were they subjective? Admittedly and necessarily so. But they got at something easily neglected; they pointed to something real. Something in need of healing within and without. Ourselves and our city.

Someone suggested they might well be used as readings to begin a neighborhood meeting. Just so. In such a paraliturgy, could they revive in others what had come alive again in us? Our love for Detroit, its people, its spirit. A realism and a vision. A sense of the times.

In that spirit, I put down here the concluding portions of my own attempt, written and rewritten. May it be a true word to the Angel of Detroit:

> *Die and arise. In your weakness is your hope. You are at an end and a beginning. Recollect your best history and come alive. You will do this if you set the lives of your people above your own. Attend to the least, the poorest, the homeless. Defend them from the ravages of corporation and economy. In their empowerment is your life. Cast off your bondages. (This too may feel like dying.) Begin with drugs and guns. Your people pray for this; join them in action. Instead of Murder Capital, become the city of nonviolence. It can be so. Your industrial heyday has gone to rust. You will not see its like again. Now think small. Encourage the modest, an economy of creativity and self-reliance. Nourish the projects of human scale, the works of community and struggle. Let your empty lots bloom green; you will find there a hidden economy all its own. Sit light upon the river, but not as real estate frontage for the rich. Be in right relationship to its life, and through it to the region, to earth itself. For your sins, enough. Now you have my blessing. Sing to glory and come to life.*

Let it be so. Amen.

1992

Stations of the Cross

Beginning in 1979 The Detroit Catholic Worker Community has annually undertaken a public liturgy, carrying a cross and walking the Good Friday "stations," through the streets of Detroit. At each place of crucifixion a meditation is read. What follows is the Introductory to the 1992 Booklet and two meditations from that walk. Later meditations appear further along in this volume.

Introduction

Today we remember the execution of Jesus upon the cross. We pray to be present there in memory and heart.

The way of the cross liturgy becomes for us a communal act of discernment. During Lent we consider: where is Christ crucified today? Each year the landscape we walk is different and distinct. Ground shifts beneath our feet. Spaces open and fill with new cries. Buildings disappear or spring up before us. The faces of victims and executioners rise up to us from a particular historical moment, in a particular place, both our own. The powers of domination and death that we recognize today are the same and not the same as before. We name them again. We name them anew.

This year, 1992, marks the 500th anniversary of the arrival of Columbus and the European powers to this hemisphere. We walk the way of the cross mindful in those 500 years of invasive exploitation, mindful of the spirit and the forms of empire.

We come confessing the temptation of all who call themselves disciples: to turn away in this hour, to scatter and hide, or at least to cover our eyes in the comfort of blindness. Our prayer is to stand with the women disciples who followed faithfully to the very foot of the cross.

Present with them, may our hearts be pierced and our eyes be opened. In this hour may the powers of domination and death be exposed, the powers military, economic, political, even religious. May we see them unmasked again in our own time by the cross of Christ.

As we walk the way of the cross through the streets of Detroit, may this traditional liturgy of devotion especially open the eyes of our hearts to all those with whom Christ suffers: the poor, the victims of violence and war, the refugees, the prisoners and those in bondage, the indigenous peoples, even the earth herself.

Station: Detroit River

"Even the beasts of the field cry out to you: for the rivers are dried up, and the fire has devoured the pastures of the plain." (Joel 1:20)

This river is a creature of God with a life and integrity of its own. Its basin connects and defines the biological region in which we reside. These same currents are pulled toward the seas that likewise surround and connect every nation under heaven. By it we are offered the cup of water, quenching our thirst. And into these waters generations of Christians have been baptized.

The Ojibwa called it *Wawiatonong*, "where the river goes round." Its shore was for them a place of meeting. And they tread lightly upon its banks.

The Europeans called it *de troit*, "the straits." It was for them a place of trading and eventually of forts that were held and fought for with warships. They made of it a border between nation states. The industrial powers saw in it a source of transportation: furs and ores and manufactured goods. With it they washed their machines, flushing away petrochemicals and waste.

The river all but died of human contempt. Like earth itself, it suffers a crucifixion all its own. Its waters flow like a wound, bearing toxins. Gasping for breath, it cries out in silent agony.

Verse: *Were you there when the waters choked with waste?*

Station: Casinos

"And they cast lots to divide his garments." (Luke 23:34)

On weekends the bridge and the tunnel to Windsor are jammed with cars. People cross the river to gamble in casinos. They stand in line to put their money in machines or hand it over in piles upon a table. The house rakes it in.

The view from Detroit is full of envy and covetousness. Good dollars are crossing the river, escaping our clutch. Here men in white shirts detail casinos on city maps, razing this or that old structure to lay a cornerstone, imagining in their hearts a new foundation for Detroit's economy.

A vision is cast: rich and poor will gather at the table, and fork over the loot. On this foundation an economy of "service" employment could be built. On this foundation the tax base may be expanded. On this foundation political careers can be made. On this foundation a ballpark would be erected. On this foundation a riverfront might be developed. The dollars will flow like streams of salvation to our city.

In truth, this foundation is built upon sand. It would be constructed on nothing. Nothing but a lie, a conjurer's trick. Nothing but addiction and corruption. Nothing but a compulsive wish, a well-marketed false hope. No goods would be produced. No true services rendered. No spirit would be nourished. No neighborhood or community would be served. No Native American sovereignty would be honored and dignified, but only reduced to a legal loophole, a marketable commodity. Even the dollars would only flow through and elsewhere away.

And when the rains fall and the floods come and the winds beat against that house, not one stone would be left upon another.

Verse: *Were you there when they sold the poor a lie?*

1994

City Life, Scenes and Feelings: Interview with Jeanie and Bill Wylie-Kellermann

Detroit Lives, Robert H. Mast, ed.
(Philadelphia: Temple University Press), 1994

JEANIE: I moved to Detroit to work for the Associated Press. I was miserable in that environment. It was the most racist and sexist place I ever had the lack of pleasure to work in. I fell in love with Detroit. My involvement in Poletown started in 1981. The first time I visited a Poletown neighborhood council meeting, the people really won my heart. They were hard-working, working class, union people who were gradually putting together a pretty sophisticated analysis of what was being done to them in the destruction of their community. I wanted to put my skills at their disposal, so I don't think I missed another meeting after that.

The resilience of the people in Poletown is one of the things that I found most striking. People were having their neighborhood decimated, houses were on fire, there was construction dust. People would come into the church center and say, "I can't breathe, I can't sleep at night." The folks in Poletown invited the daughter of the chairman of General Motors to have her wedding at the Immaculate Conception Church [then scheduled for demolition] when it became public that she was getting married. They rented a bulldozer and took it out to the house of the chairman of General Motors to let him know how it felt to have bulldozers pull up on his lawn. Once the church had been taken over by the police, they wove flowers through the fence that was between them and the church demolition. Police officers were put every twelve feet along the fence to keep people from scaling the fence to stop the demolition. The ladies went and got red vigil candles from the church that they had saved and put them beside the feet of every police officer.

The neighborhood was not saved. The Cadillac plant was built. It's not been a very productive or worthwhile plant, even from GM's perspective. Ironically, the analysts have said that the plant's too big. [Laughs] Shortly after opening the plant, they permanently laid off 17,000 Michigan workers. The City Council was quoted as saying that was a real slap in the face after all they had done for GM. But I wouldn't say the struggle in Poletown was for nothing.

Initially I worked on a documentary film *Poletown Lives!* When we were working on the film there was only a very, very small number of people who would give *any* credence to what we were saying. Most of the left was solidly behind the mayor because he had at one time been associated with the Communist Party and had not renounced it, he was the first black mayor, he had a good track record on civil rights, he had sort of a gutsy, street-talk profile that made him seem real appropriate for the city. To suggest that he was selling out the city's resources for a song to corporate interests was untenable. You just could not do it. You got laughed at in any forum. And to criticize the archdiocese was a difficult thing to do. A couple years later the archdiocese closed forty-two churches in the city and made its intentions real clear.

If any of these institutions for a moment had said, "Let's stop and look at the plant configuration and see if we can save the neighborhood and also build the plant," they'd have found out that they could. GM put a lot of pressure on them and said that it had to happen immediately. All these institutions said that GM was being civically responsible . . . . If you care about your neighborhoods it's gonna be a solo fight or a fight along with other neighborhood groups.

BILL: Being a resident of the city, a pastor, and a parent, my commitments to nonviolent resistance have more and more bridged what would be global issues and local ones. Nonviolent resistance is more urgent than ever. With changes in the Cold War and recently in the Soviet Union, there's going to be very different shape to things. The new world order is really going to be a totalizing—I was going to say totalitarian—one-system order with alternatives probably not permitted. In the past, on a global scale everyone was forced into choosing sides, East or West, but now it's really going to be First versus Third World.

JEANIE: The irony is that Detroit's probably not the place where people want to build. If corporations are going to be attracted to build in the city of Detroit it would be because there were decent schools and a strong infrastructure that made it a tenable place for their employees to work. But that's not the way the City Council and the mayor have viewed it. What the mayor in particular sees is a lot of underused land that he's perfectly willing to clear regardless of who lives on it. So they continue with these megaprojects. All these new developments along the river are touted as this tremendous boom to the city of Detroit. But those office buildings are not occupied. They lure people out of the old office buildings to become tenants at reduced rates in new ones, and the old buildings are operating on one-third occupancy, and eventually go under, and then need to be torn down. It's a pathetic idea.

I don't think there's any guarantee that we get to keep the standard of living that we've become accustomed to, as the jobs get put together in Mexico. Most Mexican workers couldn't buy them. If US workers don't have a union wage income they're not going to be able to affirm them either.

Detroit doesn't have any alternatives whatsoever. There's a whole echelon of people, probably including representatives in the federal government, who don't care if you throw Detroit away. Suburban people are often quoted as saying, "Nuke it!" Use the neutron bomb, get rid of all the people, and save some of the buildings. Given that there is very little corporate investment, I don't think Detroit has an alternative except community-based economics. Get people mobilized and independent of the current economic structure in a way that is really promising.

BILL: I think we're involved in a kind of spiritual struggle. Fundamentally, it's hope versus despair. I think despair isn't a free-floating issue of spirit, but very focused. It's the main method of political rule and economic power in Detroit. Poletown is really pivotal in that connection. I think that people live in neighborhoods around the city where large projects are slated, hovering as a sort shadow over the neighborhood. That shadow casts a huge spirit of futurelessness on a neighborhood. You can say that about City Airport, the Briggs Neighborhood here, and a number of places where these projects are hovering. We lived in the Briggs Community neighborhood, north of the expressway, off Trumbull Avenue, where a new Tiger Stadium had been proposed—

JEANIE: It reached a point there where there were all the signs of Poletown all over again: the arson, the real blockbusting. No one said, "We want to buy your house because it's going to be condemned and then we can sell it for more money than it's worth." But we began getting fliers saying "We want to buy your house." One block over, an apartment building went up in flames and sparks went over our house and caught the house behind us on fire. The area was unlivable so we got out. This was deliberate demolition policy of the city of Detroit.

BILL: At the time we were there, a church on Martin Luther King with a day care center set about to build a playground. The community actually built it. It was one of those nice playscapes that the kids had designed. Well-placed sources told the church, "Don't do it; you're wasting your money because that's where the stadium's gonna go." Now, there's an example where you're being urged not to do something because there's a plan for your neighborhood. In 1986 or '87 the newspapers were trying to get information on where the city of Detroit owned land within the city boundaries. The administration refused. The papers filed a freedom of information request. The city refused. The judge found the city in contempt. Emmett Moten, the city development director, went to *jail* to try to prevent that information from getting out. When it *finally* came out, our neighborhood was where the city owned more than anywhere else. They'd been land-banking. A house would become available or vacant. Someone, a neighbor, would try to buy it and, boom, it would not only be unavailable, but it was *demolished* immediately and you'd have an empty lot. When we left, there were only four houses on our side of the block and two on the other side.

JEANIE: The *dangerous* houses were allowed to stay, so those would stand and be hazardous for your children. The viable houses were destroyed.

BILL: I believe, at least at an unconscious level, maybe at a calculated one, that crack is used to clear neighborhoods that the city wants for development. I've talked to people who are part of WEPROS [We the People Reclaiming Our Streets], the anti-crack movement. Folks who had lived in the State Fair neighborhood experienced that years ago with heroine. We were experiencing it in the Briggs Community neighborhood. At that time I was pasturing in the Cass Corridor area. At a community meeting we asked Emmett Moten a number of questions about neighborhood development. I heard him describe what he called a police strategy, "to corral the crack houses into one neighborhood," so they could drop the net over them. Now that's not a serious police strategy.

You can see places in the city that have come to be called "the hole," where crack is very concentrated. The city wants to extend City Airport, and suddenly you have a neighborhood riddled with crack. Now I'm not saying that downtown in some office people say, "All right, send the crack in there." At an institutional level, almost at a spiritual level, there's a kind of collusion. If the cops know that this neighborhood doesn't have a future they're not gonna risk their asses for the sake of a neighborhood that isn't gonna *be* there in a year.

Poletown was a situation where arson was actually systematic and financed economically. The suggestion in Jeanie's book was that the folks who were demolishing houses would pay kids on the street to light fires cause it's easier to demolish a burned-out hulk than a full-standing house. Well, there's an economic pressure to burn the houses, but that also works to create despair in the neighborhood. I think *Devil's Night* goes back to Poletown where arson had a targeted economic base. [*Note:* Ze'ev Chafets, in his book *Devil's Night* (3–4), writes, "It was in the fall of 1986 that I first saw the devil on the streets of Detroit . . . . Three years earlier, in 1983, for reasons no one understands, America's sixth largest city suddenly erupted into flames."] Landlords use the occasion to do insurance fires.

In Detroit the spirit of the city is part of political discourse. Where is the spirit of the city? Who has it? Where is it alive and well and where is it fallen and corrupted? Those are the theological issues. The City Council gives out the Spirit of Detroit Award. The mayor uses the Spirit of Detroit as an emblem of renaissance, or whatever. On the other hand you have a coalition of neighborhood groups that fights the city over block grant priorities. It's called SOS, Save Our Spirit. The Spirit of Detroit statue downtown is a symbolic political space in the city. Demonstrations, vigils, press conferences, etc., happen with that as a backdrop. There is a sort of power to it.

JEANIE: There was a real passivity in 1980 after we had been in a recession for several years. It took several years for people to realize that this is not our average recession. This is something permanent that's changing the nature of the city.

What came from that since then are these voices of hope throughout the city. The one that's clearest and most distinct for me is SOSAD [Save Our Sons and Daughters]. To have the parents of kids who've been killed, and the parents of kids who are in jail for having done the killings, stand on the same platform and talk about the importance of our youth in the city of Detroit, is a tremendous reversal of this huge sense of despair. These small movements and voices of hope are setting up a countervailing momentum for the city of Detroit.

At a certain point, having been treated so badly and abused for so long, some of the people of Detroit, those who aren't part of an addiction cycle, have finally been able to come together and say, "We don't need the Economic Growth Corporation, we don't need the urban planning master's students who arrive in Detroit because they couldn't make it into a more glamorous city. We don't need the experts at General Motors or the folks at community economic development who say what's best for the city of Detroit. They've made a shambles of it."

The biggest question is whether or not people are going to be able to capture the imagination of the youth. The youth in Detroit, young African American males, die of murder more often than anything else. That's to be born with a death sentence. I have a good friend whose father was surprised when he made it to eighteen and said, "I thought you'd be dead or in jail." And he writes periodically about what it's like to have watched all his friends end up dead or in jail. If that's your inheritance, you know it real well by the time you're five because you've been to a variety of funerals and you watched the mothers of your friends cry. It's going to take a significant spirit to reverse that. There's always been a battle between hope and despair. Hope and despair are manipulated by the political and economic interests.

BILL: Our block here has been fighting crack houses for some time. The worst time was when we had five crack houses on the block. They were infrastructure for a sort of open drug bazaar going on in the park. There was a lot of traffic. At one point the block came together. People who had lived here for thirty years and didn't know one another's names sat around and met and undertook some public acts of solidarity as a block. Some of the houses had been burned down and empty hulks or empty lots remained. A decisive thing in changing the spirit of the block was that a number of Puerto Rican families from the same village in Puerto Rico had moved onto the block. They have a very public culture. They sit on their front porches at night or on weekends and sing. There's an ongoing fiesta. They have lots of kids. Suddenly the life of the block is a public life. The street just had a different feel to it.

JEANIE: The national media comes to Detroit to look at the city that's the furthest gone, the most destroyed, and asks, "Is this the future of the

American city?" Either this city will be totally eaten alive house by house by crack, addictive psychology, violence, abandonment, poverty, or there will be a change. There aren't any alternatives in Detroit, so community economics and community life either will, or won't, save the city because there's nothing that's going to, short of a radical change on the part of federal government.

Given the grip of current institutional arrangement of power and money, politicians don't have enough power and enough imagination to be able to make the kind of changes that are needed. They would do so at the sacrifice of their own career and very few are willing to do that. What needs to be done instead is that people in the community set the tone and agenda, and eventually the politicians will follow. With any luck, later there will be bank loans. Eventually the establishment will say that's the bandwagon they've been on all along.

If we waited for Washington, DC, we would give up in despair. There was that brief moment when there was gonna be a peace dividend because the Cold War was over. I think people had a moment of hope that they would be able to get some of those resources back into the city and create a better way of living. In no time, that money was used in Iraq. This is another opportunity to be disappointed. If there is a groundswell, if there is a community revolt, if there is a new sense of survival among people in Detroit, it would probably most quickly influence local politicians, but it eventually would affect congressional representatives and senators. They wouldn't *not* be able to be influenced by it.

1995

Reading the Building, Seeing the Powers

EXCERPTED FROM *DYING HUMANLY:*
THE RESURRECTED LIFE OF JEANIE WYLIE

One time during a large picket around the newspaper headquarters, I noticed high above the street, nearly out of sight and mind, epithets etched in stone, ringing the façade above. I pointed them out to Jeanie, and we read as we circled. Later at the rally in front of the edifice, I took the microphone and asked, "Have you ever read the *Detroit News* building?"

It was a confusing moment for the strikers. Then I pointed aloft and began to utter the names, among them: Friend of Every Righteous Cause, Reflector of Every Human Interest, Mirror of the Public Mind, Dispeller of Ignorance and Prejudice, Bond of Civic Unity, Protector of Civic Rights, Troubler of Public Conscience, Scourge of Evil Doers, Exposer of Secret Iniquities, Unrelenting Foe of Privilege and Corruption, A Light Shining in All Dark Places.

Were these intentions a pretense from the beginning, a mere "facade" covering the machinery of power and profit—or did they publicly remember the true vocation, the calling of a community newspaper? In Jeanie's and my biblical reading, every structure of power with a life and integrity of its own, every "principality and power," is called by God to serve the human community in particular ways, notably in this case by being a servant of the truth, and even justice.

These phrases written in stone, romantic and pretentious as they were, actually suggested the very bases on which Detroit Newspapers Incorporated stands before the judgment of God.

As I read out each one at the rally, the strikers laughed. Their laughter identified the incongruity. It signaled their theological understanding of the fall.

The *News* was indeed a "troubler of the public conscience," but in a way exactly opposite of that intended. It had become the trouble, when it should instead be the conscience. I noted that Turner of Profit was not even mentioned in the auspicious list. Neither was Master of Marketing, Doctor of Spins, nor Twister of Truth—let alone Buster of Unions. This is to say that in the fall, the vocation of a newspaper becomes distorted or even inverted. It gets turned upside down.

Instead of serving the community, it imagines the community exists to serve the interests of the newspaper. It puts profit before both readers and workers. It has contempt for both, actually assaulting the community. That is the reality of the fall. The work of redemption in that moment had to do with exposing the lie, rebuking the distortion, and calling the papers back to their creaturely purposes. If you think about the work of Readers United from this standpoint, you'll notice that we were also exercising the same discernment with the unions, recognizing them as creaturely powers.

The New York Times may have been premature, but in the end it wasn't wrong. We did lose that strike. It slipped away in whimpers. That's a source of grief in our life. Certainly for the workers who lost cars and homes. Some fell off the twelve-step wagon, and others saw marriages go belly-up from the strain.

But you also had to grieve for Detroit, a union town taking another hit, "Murder City" losing another of its lives. The dailies never fully recovered their circulation as they'd presumed. And, to be honest, more than a decade later, I still can't bring myself to subscribe.

1996

Readers Before Profits

SOJOURNERS MAGAZINE, JANUARY/FEBRUARY, 1996

> *These corporations have no loyalty to the city of Detroit, no respect for our culture as a union town, no concern for the Detroit strikers and their families who are in danger of losing their homes as the strike drags on.* —Grace Lee Boggs, *community activist*

It has struck me more than once how thoroughly our response to the newspaper strike ongoing in Detroit has been shaped by a theological comprehension of the principalities and powers. It proves both illuminating and practical.

The situation is this: last July, six unions representing 2,600 workers were forced to strike when the company demanded another round of deep job cuts and refused to operate under the old contracts while bargaining new. Almost immediately it announced the hiring of "permanent replacement workers."

"The company" in this case comprises the two largest newspaper conglomerates in the country. Gannett, owner of the *Detroit News* (not to mention *USA Today*), holds eighty-one other papers, by which it made profits last year of $636 million. Just a week after the strike began, Gannett initiated purchase of Multimedia Inc. for $1.6 billion. The *Detroit Free Press*, meanwhile, is owned by Knight-Ridder, which has twenty-seven other newspapers and took $170 million in profit for 1994.

Together their business operations are fused in a "Joint Operating Agreement," which preempts competition, reduces the work force, presents a single bargaining front, and last year earned profits of a million dollars a week.

It's clear the conglomerates are prepared to expend (pretax) losses of more than $100 million to bust the unions. That expense is already paying off in Philadelphia and Miami, where they are exacting substantial concessions.

In a long front-page article on November 11, *The New York Times* essentially declared victory for the company. The announcement was premature. This is an important strike. And the wider union movement knows it. The election of activists John Sweeney and Richard Trumka to AFL-CIO leadership has already yielded commitments of funds, staff, and vision. It may be a truly long haul.

The theological question that we have been asking publicly is both simple and quite radical: what is the vocation of a newspaper? All principalities are called to praise God and serve human life. In this case, specifically, that service is to the larger Detroit community by shedding the light of truth, by facilitating communication and public conversation. This, indeed, is discernibly the calling to which the paper is held accountable in the judgment of God.

In the distortion of sin and the fall, however, that vocation of service becomes confused, preempted, or inverted. The newspapers serve first and foremost the corporate chains, absentee owners with no stake in or commitment to the community, conglomerates who imagine the vocation of a newspaper is little more than to clear 15 percent profit. In that demonic confusion, truth or discourse become a matter of indifference, contempt for their workers is one with a contempt for their readers. Frankly, this is a pattern that may be recognized all across the country.

To frame the question as Jesus once did: were the newspapers made for human beings (the community, readers, workers), or were human beings made for the newspapers? The slogan "readers before profits" becomes a theological aphorism in this light, no?

Readers United (RU), a group that's been formed virtually out of meetings in our living room, has taken that phrase as its organizational maxim in attempting to be an independent voice of the community within this labor struggle. It was amazing how eager people have been to identify with the project or lend us their names. In a series of public demonstrations—one where we dramatically burned the scab papers, section by section—we have tried to broaden and reframe the issues at the front door of the company, particularly the matter of their role as members and servants of this community. In that light we've rebuked their bad faith bargaining, violence, and contempt for the workers.

While the company daily runs slick commercials attacking the striking workers and their unions, we are organizing toward a citywide forum for early in the year to keep reiterating the fundamental point: what is a newspaper, and how does the community hold it accountable to its calling?

One tactic and handle of accountability we've just begun to reflect upon is the corporation charter. There is, of course, no mention of corporations in the Constitution. They assume the status of "persons" and a legal right to protection of life, liberty, and property under a 1886 court ruling initiated by the railroads. Ironically (to say the least) that ruling was predicated on the Fourteenth Amendment, just then ratified to protect the rights of freed slaves!

Historically, corporation charters were granted by states for limited and fixed terms to be renewed only if the corporation could demonstrate that it was fulfilling its purposes (its vocation). Previously, corporations were prohibited from owning other corporations. Nor could they participate in the electoral process, financially or otherwise. Today every state (except Alaska) retains a charter revocation clause.

We are asking: is it possible that this could be an avenue for reclaiming community accountability over the conglomerates? As Grace Lee Boggs of the RU steering group puts it, "We need a landmark decision in the mounting conflict between the interests of local communities and absentee corporations which will do for today's movement what *Brown v. Kansas Board of Education* did for the civil rights movement."

Readers United has also pushed the vocational question with the unions themselves. Since a newspaper, being part of the community's life, is a substantially different product than steel or cars, the strike itself must be fought in a distinctive way. Asking readers, for example, to boycott the scab papers (even the company acknowledges circulation is down 25 percent) is to leave them in the dark concerning crucial local news—some with urgent political implications. It's not only strategically smart, but part of the unions' responsibility to the community to provide a genuine newspaper, at least for the duration of the strike.

This we have said in letters and leaflets, face-to-face conversations, and news interviews—recirculating a practical proposal made in midsummer. Finally, just before Thanksgiving, *The Sunday Journal* became a reality. So now? Now we urge broader community editorial participation. We urge the paper to be more than just a strike tactic, but likewise to honor fully the vocation of a newspaper.

This is to say, we are not unmindful that unions are principalities as well, called under the sovereignty of God to serve human life by serving their members' interests, by honoring the worth and dignity of all human labor, and by risking themselves in engagement with the commercial powers. And they too have a responsibility to the community.

However, in the fall that vocation also gets corrupted. Unions may become more preoccupied with institutional survival and self-preservation than with the human needs of their members. Leadership may serve other interests in pursuit of reelection or be more concerned with guarding the coffer than with justice. Readers United stands with the striking workers, but all the while voicing a call that the unions too be servants of the community.

Violence remains the toughest issue. I speak of that initiated by the company, first the structural violence assaulting people's lives and jobs, but more directly violence on the picket line, especially where workers have tried to block vehicles from delivering company papers. Repeatedly, trucks have driven into crowds of strikers, resulting in a number of injuries.

Often as not those trucks are driven by Vance Security, the Pinkerton-like, paramilitary force hired by the company. Vance, which came into its own during the 1989 mine workers strike, advertises itself as specially skilled in documenting (by photo and video evidence) the violence of strikers in order to secure injunctions (the company managed to get one forthwith) and to portray violence as the tactic of protesters.

I have been present when riot-equipped forces charge or posture to provoke a reaction, filming from the roof. Driving a truck into an angry crowd does draw sticks and rocks, equally photogenic. The company's ubiquitous commercials "deplore striker violence" (in order to mask its own). Some of them show burning vehicles that I believe were actually set afire by their own security.

Yet the unions have been slow to embrace disciplined nonviolent action (after the pattern of the United Mine Workers, for example).[1] An

---

1. See Wylie-Kellermann, "Unions and Communities," 9.

ambitious plan of escalating nonviolent action, prepared last August, was cast aside when the injunction came down and the trucks ran the crowds. Moreover, the most creative and militant caucus among the strikers adheres to the slogan "By any means necessary."

One witness of nonviolence has been Bishop Tom Gumbleton, of the Catholic Archdiocese of Detroit, who has been active from the beginning, heading up statements by religious leaders, speaking publicly and in the media, testifying against company violence on the line, confronting and mediating with the police. In his connection with Readers United, he has met with union leadership to urge the production of a strike paper and to exhort a disciplined nonviolent approach that could include religious-based direct action.

To my mind the question hanging fire remains: will the unions embrace a thoroughgoing strategy of this sort or will the nonviolent initiative need be seized entirely by groups in the community like Readers United?

1998

To the Hoop Dance: A Grieving Rite

The San Antonio Current,
March 26–April 1, 1998, No. 411, 10–13.

The version here is the subsequent version, "In Courts Divine: My Life in the Game," *Detroit Metro Times,* April 1–7, 2009

The only record of Michael Jordan's that I've ever broken is the number of times I've come out of basketball retirement. About to turn sixty, I'm once again back at a weekly game running full court, at least till I feel a hamstring twinge and have the wisdom to step off for the night.

 Years ago when I thought my quit was for good, I ached with the loss. I fretted and fumed. My sweet wife, Jeanie, said, "You need a grieving ritual!" When I set out to write a poem, it turned into an essay, my life and times in the game.

 I started it just turning a basketball in my hands, worn and wonderful, and offering a prayer of sorts. Not for victory—I've never done that even when my coach would nod to me piously for a Cooley High School pre-game moment. Then and there—only for our best, for safety, for teamwork, even for the other guys. But here—for letting go, for putting aside this game with grace.

 The ball with a life of its own, however, summons round memory.

My dad, also a Methodist pastor (you know, I think he played in seminary), always served churches with gymnasiums, my private courts in the house of God, where hours alone (or with my three younger brothers) could yield an unconscious lay-up, the leaping steps of which I'd rehearse again on every passage through our living room archway.

Once on a visit, our cousins (not really ballplayers themselves) brought a family movie camera. The gym (most everyone else at church called it the "All Purpose Room") became a set. We edited stop action on the fly to enact the impossible: full court swishes, slam dunks from a step ladder, and magic passes with a reappearing ball. We fancied ourselves six foot eight. We were in a Globetrotter's dream. The footage, now a precious eight millimeter heirloom, never did justice to our imaginings.

I remember, even the smell of it, putting on my first real uniform—a junior high treasure of gold and black, slightly coarse, and aged enough to hint of tradition—then watching the dividing wall fold and draw back like a curtain on an honest full court with glass boards, the pep band playing jazz as if it were a march, and the aroma of popcorn drifting out from the bleachers. Those stiff white cheers ("Do like the Navy does, sink it") gave way in high school to liquid and rhythmic ones, full of street soul and a crowd swinging in unison, background music for the run and gun dance. We're talking the mid-sixties and Cooley High School.

Actually, my coach taught the fundamentals, the patterns of flow, as though they were waltz steps pasted to the floor. More help in an odd way was Abe Eliowitz, one of my football coaches (who still holds, beyond his dying day, the Big Ten punt record at Michigan). Off-season in the gym he threw soft pinpoint spirals drawing my fingertips a stretch farther with each. It was an over-the-shoulder skill made for the fast break game.

But I learned most from George Johnson, a year my elder. (I was to be captain; he was too "undisciplined," too quick to laugh, too rhythmic to his bones, to even start.) He gave me a stutter dribble crossover, demonstrated the quick first step, and a two-handed Cazzie Russell board shot inside. When twenty-five years later he showed up homeless and overweight, waxing incoherent, a used-up, drug-treated Vietnam vet, I took him home to sleep on the couch, went upstairs, and wept.

There were also opposite numbers, opponent guards I faced and knew and even stayed in touch with. During a scrimmage game with Southwestern I knocked heads with Henderson diving together for the ball. As if from a faucet, blood poured to the floor straight from my forehead. Examining me in the office, his coach allowed that a couple butterflies of tape would hold the wound for healing, but my dad fetched me to our doctor who took one look and demurred. He called a plastic surgeon already en route to a black tie affair, who, wearing a tux in the emergency room at Sinai, rolled up his sleeves and put in eighty small stitches.

Cross town on the east side those years Spencer Haywood and Ralph Simpson held court in a league all their own—beginning a run straight to state championship.

One time, a game at Henry Ford High School, to Coach's chagrin and my panic, I forgot my shoes. There I was pacing the locker room sockfoot till after the JV game to borrow some ten and a half All Stars. To this day I have a recurrent anxiety dream about some game or other beginning without me while I search madly in lockers or heading off elsewhere in a hurried quest after my shoes. My other b-ball dream, of course, is playing in the "zone"—all my moves and shots clean, smooth, and literally "unconscious." It's a sensation akin to a dream of flying.

Honestly, after high school I recall the surprise delight at playing college intramurals—no coach on the sideline crashing a clipboard to the floor like doom's crack of judgement—so no tentativeness against the cringe of misstep. Set free-wheeling and loose, I got better.

As a seminarian in New York, I ran the floor with a regular group of guys in the undercroft of Riverside Church. I may be making this up, but I think they had another gym, more worn, accessible at street level for the neighborhood kids. Frankly, we never questioned the privilege. The good court was past security, deep in silence below the nave. There I learned a fast break move running straight at the defender, awaiting the last second to drop my shoulder, slide stepping on by to the left. It stayed in my repertoire.

About the same time my best friend's buddy was trying to make it in the New York dance scene. In a darkened gym on the lower west side, he had us walk him through several play patterns and moves. He taught a rank of dancers the distinctive lanky walk of Phil Jackson, then playing forward for the Knicks, (they were a stitch all ambling in unison) and choreographed a performance called "Pick and Roll." It was so lovely he saw dance in the game.

Once Randels and I walked onto a Michigan neighborhood playground in search of a pick-up game. Two young brothers (loose, lean, and confident) sized us up: sure, they'd give us a shot. Everything clicked inside and out: off the ball moves, picks and tips and fall away jumpers. We were a sustained lopsided surprise. Thanking them and walking away, we overheard, "They old, but they good." We claimed it for a refrain.

In jail (I've landed there with some frequency for nonviolent direct action) basketball is a certain realm of freedom. Whether it's a skiddy linoleum floor indoors or a chain-link hoop in the wire-topped yard, the ball is a delight akin to a bootlegged cup of real coffee, nearly as welcome as a visit. (Actually, I was once in a fancy modular DC lockup—in the early eighties—where a half-court hoop was permanently accessible to the day room. If there must be prisons, this is an architecture that ought to be more common, for my money). In old Macomb County where we never left the rock, we made a "ball" of wadded socks and shot into a trash can on the upper bunk, working up a sweat in what surely was a dangerously physically close-quarters game. Inside, basketball was often my quick ticket to acceptance. I always delighted if I got tagged with a court nickname like "Cooley" or "Hands." Once in Oakland County Jail I crossed the rock boss early on by intervening in a late night sexual harassment of a young kid. He started giving me the evil eye, and I was beginning to cringe. Then in the yard we played opposite for one game—and thereafter he made certain we were teamed together. After my first baseline dish to him, all was forgiven.

Into my middle-aged era there was the Coach Gus Macker All World Three on Three Call Your Own Fouls Backyard Basketball Tournament. My brothers and I (usually with no more than one reunion practice, relying wholly on melding via memory of hours on hours years past) played in the early originals of that campy event now swelled to a 100,000-person extravaganza with well-organized local spin-offs and imitators. For us these were nothing less than annual family reunions replete with grandparents, aunts, and cousins decked in sunglasses and lawn chairs, with coolers of potato salad and Mountain Dew in tow. Though we lacked the necessary killer instinct, if Pauly hit from the perimeter and Stevie put the body on their big guy, we could shine, and have a few quirky trophies to show for it.

Not many years ago, I equivocated about playing in a Macker, and my brothers exercised their option to sign a replacement. When I second-guessed myself and tried to get back in, my successor, declining to step graciously aside, was upheld by the brothers to my wounded utter astonishment. At forty-four, my court career was liminal. Would this have been my last Macker? I cried. The tears released a flood of sibling history. I agonized over rivalry and exclusion and domination, wounds and wants and karmic reversals, self-doubt so deep I wondered if I was loved. Yikes, what freight this game may bear! It is the stuff of dreams, both dark and light.

There was another time of tears. Home for Christmas, the brothers commandeered yet another church gym for after dinner two on two. When Jimmy's knee, which had been through a round of surgery, locked on a rebound landing, he lay on the floor in agony. Fetching ice from the kitchen, the other three of us cried as well, partly in sympathy, but mainly for knowing we had just played all together for the last time in our lives. (In point of fact, during a season of weight-lifting and physical therapy, he started taking a few shots, entered on a few "easy" games, and before we knew it, in an idiocy common to such passions, he made a comeback for one more Macker.)

One time I myself lay on the floor writhing in pain. A rambunctious rebound had landed a finger in my eye. I was a rushing mix of emotions, anger and fear both, though honestly I'm not sure if I was more worried that I would lose the sight of my left eye or that the injury would end my career prematurely. It did preempt a trip to California. I was to fly out the next day to help lead an event at a fancy coastal retreat house, but the doctors put the nix on pressure changes of altitude. The force had not only traumatized the eyeball, but broken the tiny muscle that closes my iris. It affects my reading to this day and I now invariably wear shades outdoors. Though I walked around displacing anger for weeks, I finally had to make peace with the breaks of the game. For a while I added goggles to my equipment bag and probably played with an even more reckless abandon.

I think on a history of wounds and devices. Ordinary ones like scrapes and floor burns and huge blisters we used to puncture with a needle dipped in alcohol. After the eighty-stitch plastic surgery, I wore a hockey helmet for the remainder of the season. Prone to ankle sprains as I grew older, I learned the value of pregame stretching and a plastic air cast in my shoe became standard equipment. Coming back from the first orthoscopic knee surgery, I was fitted with a brace of space-age metal and velcro. I came to feel like robo-guard buckling up my armor for battle. In the end, surgery to the other knee punctuated my career with another period. It seemed like I was facing a choice between squeezing out maybe six more months on the court (no small consideration), or being able to take long walks with my wife, Jeanie, when we grew old (no real choice when it came down to it—but not so easy nonetheless.) When she crossed over to God three years ago it broke my heart. And here I am recklessly back on the court.

When I quit, I miss it too much. It's not like the hyped affection of NBA or Final Four commercials. In fact, sometimes I could barely watch televised games for the ache that's called up. I yearn for that Zen dance, moving and counter-moving in community. (My most frustrating days on the court were not so much when I'm missing shots as when I can't feel the flow, or worse when there's no flow to find.) In that regard, I was never really a smart player, because there was a level of thinking I just let go. I'd lose track of the score or the time or the number of fouls—nearly everything was in the movement. I know it engaged a different part of my brain because often I'd step off the floor having organized an essay or thought through a sermon, almost without realizing.

Every time I quit, I so miss that dance. And I miss my partners. Think about it: a standing weekly game in Detroit for as long as I can remember. A form of community. First, late night at Detroit Central Methodist where a group of law students (some with college ball experience) traded security duty for a sprawling apartment adjacent to the fourth-floor gym. Then at the Western YMCA (now boarded up) where you had to break into the game ("Can I run with ya?") and then hope to hold the court. Then, for eight years or more at Messiah Episcopal's crackerbox half-court where repair of the hoop from strain of the street slam-jammers could be a weekly ritual with Jimmy Sweeney hoisted aloft, tools in hand. Now at Spirit of Hope Church on Martin King and Trumbull. What a circle of friends with whom I would be so frequently and share so much in our after-game cups. Beloved memory and the stuff of dreams

So I wrote it all down for the sake of my heart, for honoring, for evocation, for purge. And this is it more or less. I hold the ball again. Naming a few names in what goes round as intercession of sorts:

My Dad, and the gift of hands,
Jimmy, Stevie, Pauly;
Hondorp, McLean, Scott, Tim, Brian, Eric, Randy;
George, Johnny, Regie, Jeff, Frank, Greg, Doug, Bill, Walter, Danny, Vernon, Gerald, and Oliver;
Bill, Don, Tom, Dale, and Tom;
Randels, Jack, John, Doug, Martin, Steve;
Mel, James, Johnny Moore, Dee, Cadillac, John, Joe Green;
The Rock Boss (whose name I can't recall) and cell mates;
Brothers Bill and Bob, Paul V. O. and the law crew;
Artie, John, Ched, Jack, Judy, Bob, Jim, Dan, J. R., Joe;

Glen, Jimmy, Jerry, Richard, Tasso, Erik, George, Sam, Herb, Tom.
Andy, Mike, Tim . . . . All the McEvoy clan at Christ the King
Now, AO, Maddie, Cisco, Phil, Danny, Jeff, John, Jim, Shawn . . . .
More than I can name . . .
To you all, thanks and common love. Bill

2002

Station: A Slot Machine Economy—MGM/Tiger Stadium

"*And they cast lots to divide his garments.*" (Luke 23:34)

For the rich with venture capital, for those who play the markets, and for so many more who simply entrust savings and futures to mutual funds and the like, an overheated economy is like casino economics. All they see is the cash flow upon the table or flooding from the mouth of a slot machine. They know not what they do. Decisions are made in an insular money world whose logic is growth, market expansion, and unlimited profit. Unseen, unknown, practically unimagined, is the living world affected: namely human communities.

They pull the lever of the global economy and capital moves at the speed of light . . . elsewhere: across town, south of the border, to another part of the planet. As capital flows are more and more unrestricted, industrial cities like Motor City see their traditional manufacturing base disappear. They find themselves grasping as their traditional manufacturing base disappears. They find themselves grasping at phantoms, seeking to become "tourist cities" or at least cities with a world-class "tourist bubble" of ball parks, convention centers, theaters, hotels . . . and, yes, casinos.

We stand before MGM Grand. We will shortly go west on Michigan to Trumbull, toward Tiger Stadium, empty, cold, and forgotten. And we'll see the lights from the new stadium, Comerica Park, not far away. Only shortly before the plan for the park was announced, Tiger Stadium had been renovated. The closest seats in baseball were not abandoned for lack of its facilities, but for the sake of the concentrated "tourist bubble," a self-contained entertainment monopoly connected by train to the convention center. "They paved paradise and put up a parking lot . . ." and when their parking lot did not make enough money for them to be satisfied, (or when others shared in the parking revenue) they simply moved the capital. The spirit of the old stadium rich with history and memory now is emptied, and the old pavement gone cold.

Elsewhere, within the bubble, an economy of "service" employment jobs is being conjured. Driving cabs, mixing drinks and waiting tables, shuffling cards and carrying chips, selling pizza and hot dogs, cleaning rooms and toilets, making beds and parking cars, endlessly guarding the doors as security. An economy of sorts. September 11? When terror cools tourism, such jobs and people as these are first affected. Verse: *Were you there when the soldiers threw the dice?*

2004

A Jazz Opera on Detroit Pastor-Organizer

ON THE EDGE, DETROIT CATHOLIC WORKER, 2004[2]

"Forgotten," a jazz musical about a pastor/organizer who was murdered at the Ford Rouge Plant, will have its world premiere at Marygrove College, March 5–7. This thing is full of history and heart. It will garner a huge viewing from the labor community, but church folk—and friends of the Worker in particular—should be attentive to this, a story close to our own as it were.

Coming to Detroit from Iowa, Lewis Bradford served as assistant at Detroit Central Methodist under Dr. Frederich Fisher, who had himself been a bishop in India, there befriended and influenced by Gandhi. After the fashion of the worker-priests, Bradford went to work in the plant. As he wrote in his diary, the "real reason" for being in Detroit was that he should "make a guided approach toward meeting the spiritual need of Detroit. This should be done at present, through [my] work, not as an evangelist."

This was the 1930s and the Depression (capital D) was taking peoples lives on the streets of Detroit and the Hoovervilles down by its tracks. Bradford began a radio show, called "The Forgotten Man's Radio Hour," innovatively interviewing people about their lives and the times as they waited in the soup line on Howard Street. In "Forgotten," Bradford sings, "When you tell your story/ Hard times are easier to bear/ Step up to the

---

2. Versions of this review also appeared in *The Michigan Citizen* and *Fellowship Magazine* (September 2004).

microphone/ If you've got something to share." Historically it is the same moment that Peter Maurin and Dorothy Day were beginning to peddle T*he Catholic Worker* from the Bowery soup lines to the streets of New York.

Bradford's own story in this jazz opera weaves through our city's remarkable history: the Ford Hunger March, the sit-down strikes, the battle of the overpass, the company campaign of terror against the union organizing efforts, and the efforts to divide the workers racially—all figure in.

And yet, practically in biblical fashion, the larger historical drama is inseparable from the deeply personal one. Over his sleeping daughter, Bradford sings, "How can I explain to you/ the work I am called to do?/ Healing wounds is my goal/ the world is crying out to be made whole/ You are a child, you need to dream/ You have not seen what I have seen/ We've got to change the world/ For me and for you/ And that's the work I'm called to do." (To take the story another level of personal, I happily confess that Steve Jones, the play's author-composer, recently told me and my daughter, Lydia, that he wrote this song after sitting at our dining room table and hearing the story of a letter I wrote to her from Bay County Jail on a two-month bit for a Wurtsmith AFB action back when Lydia was three!)

In the musical, as push came to shove in the plant, Lewis Bradford struggles with and faces his own vocation and the fullness of freedom demanded. "It's about time/ About time to take a stand/ What more do you need? We've got to work hand in hand/ The time is now, the place is here/ It's about time to break the cycle of fear."

Muriel Lester, a founder of the Fellowship of Reconciliation and a socialist from England, figures into the story at a decisive point. This was a period when the auto companies were investing in what came to be the Axis powers. An early wave of corporate globalization. If Hitler had won the war, they would have come out impeccably Nazi, I suppose. Lester led a series of meetings to which Bradford was drawn. She had just come from the far east and was traveling the world to bring attention to the atrocities committed by the Japanese in the infamous Rape of Nanking in China. As she put it, "I will try to make Americans see their own share of the guilt. They are making large profits out of supplying the means of death and torture." She wanted to talk directly with Henry Ford—and Bradford spent a day trying, in the face of active hostility, to open the door. A week later, he was dead.

On November 27, 1937 Bradford was found fatally injured in an obscure and lonely part of the plant. The company insisted it was an industrial accident, a fall. So said the obituary and others kept a judicious silence. His wife and daughter were told not to ask questions and urged to leave town. They did.

Here's where the story beneath the story comes into play, yet another level of the personal. Sixty years later, Steve Jones, a jazz musician living in Washington, DC, and a relative of Lewis Bradford, encounters the unresolved contradiction, the nagging question filtering down in family history: was he in fact murdered? And thus begins a personal and spiritual (and ultimately musical) journey of his own. Immersing himself in Detroit labor history, locating Bradford's lost journal in an attic, and above all getting hold of the autopsy report (thereby hangs a tale of its own) from which a forensic pathologist in the Wayne County Medical Examiner's office has confirmed, "This was no accident—this was a homicide that was never investigated.... There's no way in hell that he fell."

As the pieces of the story became backlit one at a time, Jones began processing them musically and before he knew it the opera was emerging at the piano beneath his fingertips—in the chords and idiom of his own heart.

He tells a story of courage and struggle. But, like the Gospels themselves, it is also a story of the Powers That Be, and Jones is not afraid to name names. Henry Ford sings, as though right off the canvas of a Diego Rivera portrait. And Harry Bennett, Ford's enforcer and heir apparent, utters his own dark song. Then there's Father Coughlin, whose own radio show foils "The Forgotten Man's Hour," and presages the era of hate broadcasting.

In the end it is a story of recovered memory and even resurrection faith. The chorus invokes Joe Hill. "Don't mourn. Organize," says he. And of Bradford: "We remember you/ We remember you/ What you gave/ What you've done/ Will not be Forgotten."

It is an act of memory that Catholic Workers would do well to share. The nagging questions of history summon us. Not to mention the One in whom all martyrs are gathered and remembered.

2005

Station: Energy Policy, Auto, and War

Jesus turned to them and said, "Daughters of Jerusalem, do not weep for me. Weep for yourselves and for your children." (Luke 23:28)

Verse: *Were you there when they traded blood for oil?*

On February 16 of this year, the Kyoto treaty on global warming went into effect in most developed nations in the world—with the exception of the United States. There is widespread agreement among scientists today that climate change, caused by greenhouse gas emissions from fossil fuel consumption, is seriously endangering life on our planet. Consequences may include species extinction; increasingly severe storms, floods, and droughts; the death of the oceans. A recent report commissioned by the US Defense Department warned that abrupt climate change could bring the planet to the edge of anarchy, as food, water, and energy supplies dwindle. Many experts warn that the threat to global security is far greater than that of terrorism. Yet in the face of that this threat, the Bush Administration has actively worked to discredit climate science and block international efforts to address the problem.

US dependence on oil has already led us into a disastrous war and occupation in Iraq. With less than 5 percent of the world's population, we consume more than 25 percent of global oil production. Transportation, which burns nearly two-thirds of US oil, is "the key to cutting oil dependence," a

Rocky Mountain Institute report states. Improving the average household vehicle fleet mileage by thirteen miles per gallon would displace all of the oil we import from the Persian Gulf. As one commentator asks: "Did we put our kids in 0.5 miles-per-gallon tanks and 17 feet-per-gallon aircraft carriers because we failed to put them in 33 miles-per-gallon cars?"

2006

Station: Commodification of Water

"I thirst." A jar full of sour wine was standing there. So they put a sponge full of the wine on a branch of hyssop and held it out to his mouth. (John 19:28–9)

The United Nations names access to potable water a basic human right.

To be cut of from it is a form of crucifixion.

Today in the land of Jesus, in Galilee and the Occupied Territories, the control of water is indeed a life and death issue. A wall cuts off people and their crops from access. In the southwest USA, states fight and sue one another over river water. In response to global warming, they plan new water capture projects totaling $2.5 billion. Around the world water is being fought over; it is a resource that is everywhere being privatized and commodified.

Thomas Merton prophesied that the day may yet be when "rain becomes a utility that they can plan and distribute for money. By 'they' I mean the people who . . . think that what has no price has no value, that what cannot be sold is not real, so that the only way to make something real is to place it on the market. The time will come when they will sell you even your rain" *(Raids on the Unspeakable)*.

This river, fed by the rains and flowing freely, is connected as one with all the waters of the world. It is the source of water for all in its basin. Upstream, intake and purification is done by the City of Detroit.

Yet last year 40,000 homes had their water shut off by the Detroit Water Board. This in a city with an unemployment rate of 19 percent, where 33 percent of the population lives below the poverty line. When water is cut off, low-income people are not merely inconvenienced, they lose their children to Protective Services. Their health fails. Their lives spiral out of control.

Though proposals have been put forward to reduce water rates for those with lessened ability to pay, no such plan has been implemented. Water rates have been raised again across the board. The head of the water department who has accelerated these shutoffs of the poor, has been rewarded by the mayor, his a salary raised to over a quarter million dollars per year.

Let justice roll down in the waters. Let those who say, I thirst, come without cost.

Verse: *Were you there when he thirsted with the poor?*

2007

Station: Detroit River—Undocumented Workers

In his flesh Christ has made both groups into one and has broken down the dividing wall of hostility between us . . . thus making peace, and reconciling both groups to God in one body through the cross . . . . So then you are no longer strangers and aliens, but you are citizens with the saints and also members of the household of God.
(Eph 2:14, 19)

By the waters of Detroit, we stand at the border as US plans are afoot to add either a second span to the Ambassador Bridge, or build a new billion-dollar crossing further south in Delray with a 100-acre plaza for trucks alone. At the border, capital can cross at the speed of light. Commodities move at will under Free Trade agreements. But human beings have a harder go. Your papers please. On our southern border we build not bridges but walls—a barbed-wire construction intended to force people who cross, into the deadliest of wilderness.

In Detroit, undocumented workers are declared "illegal" persons; they are harassed and denied basic human rights. Profiled by language, they suffer arbitrary regulations withholding simple identification for driving or check cashing. Their communities are subjected to constant surveillance. As employees, they work and then are routinely denied pay. Or are injured and promptly turned out without compensation or health care. If they complain or organize, Immigration and Customs Enforcement (ICE) appears.

ICE, formerly INS, but now of Homeland Security, is the economic enforcer, keeping a whole population vulnerable to economic exploitation. In effect, they terrorize the community. We name this violence. It is violence to tear families apart, breaking up communities with removal or inducing intra-family violence under stress of repression. It is violence to raid homes in the dark of night and disappear people; to imprison without access to representation; to stand as a constant threat of deportation, enforcing their susceptibility to economic abuse.

In economic function and effect, ICE does in immigrant communities what the Klan has historically done in the south. Any church worth the salt of its tears must ask: where shall they find sanctuary? Where shall these aliens and strangers find citizenship in the body?

Verse: *Were you there when they took me in the night?*

2009

Resurrection City: How Detroit Comes Alive in the New Depression

SOJOURNERS, VOL. 38 NO. 5, MAY 2009

I don't think of myself as peculiarly prescient or enjoying the gift of discernment. But twenty years ago in these pages I wrote an article about my beloved city, attempting to get at its ethos and moment, its life and integrity as a spiritual power (see the earlier chapter, "Discerning the Angel of Detroit.") After the fashion of John's letters to the angels of the seven churches in Revelation 2, it concluded with these portions of my own letter to Detroit's Angel:

> *Die and arise. In your weakness is your hope. You are at an end and a beginning. Recollect your best history and come alive. You will do this if you set the lives of your people above your own. Attend to the least, the poorest, the homeless. Defend them from the ravages of corporation and economy. In their empowerment is your life. Cast off your bondages. (This too may feel like dying.) Begin with drugs and guns. Your people pray for this; join them in action. Instead of Murder Capital, become the city of nonviolence. It can be so. Your industrial heyday has gone to rust. You will not see its like again. Now think small. Encourage the modest, an economy of creativity and self-reliance. Nourish the projects of human scale, the works of community and struggle. Let your empty lots bloom green; you will find there a hidden economy all its own. Sit light upon the river, but not as real estate frontage for the rich. Be in right relationship*

> to its life, and through it to the region, to earth itself. For your sins, enough. Now you have my blessing. Sing to glory and come to life.

That's actually a good and true word. Truer even for now than then.

What if Detroit, the vacated and rusting shell of a de-industrialized city, turns out to be the hustling forefront of urban sustainability? Another city is possible in the shell of the old. For those with eyes to see, it's actually happening.

In a certain sense Detroit has been living in the decades since with the implosion and collapse that is finally catching up with the rest of the country, and with the global system for that matter. In four decades we went from being the city with the highest rate of home ownership in the nation to being the city with the highest foreclosure rate. We lost a million people, mostly white folks. Of homes in Detroit about a fifth are vacant or abandoned. And still homeless people camp in parks and under bridges. As much as white flight, capital flight, and job flight took their tolls. In the last decade nearly a quarter million auto-related jobs disappeared in the Metro area. Do you find the prospect of double-digit unemployment daunting? That we've had for a long time—percentage wise we're currently in the twenties.

And yet. The roots beneath are full of life. Amidst signs of death an urban resurrection is afoot. In all these things there are openings and spaces for a whole new way of doing city life.

CASINO ECONOMIES?

Not that "*de troit*" (the city by the "the straits"), living in dire straits, hasn't taken some detours. Casino economics has certainly been a temptation. Twenty year ago I noted that the city's working-class spirit was a collaborator in resisting the incursion of the high-glitz casino "industry." If so, it eventually caved to the seductions of necessity, as it were. At the peak of the casino struggle, Mayor Young challenged the resisters, community and religious, to come up with an economic alternative. That would prove a prophetic taunt.

Meanwhile we currently suffer three permanent casinos, though one of them is about to throw in its cards and fold. They do provide a certain number of "jobs." A couple years back 26,000 people lined up for 1,000 positions at the MGM Grand. But is it an economy? An industry which produces nothing, unless you consider its addictive drug of choice, adrenaline—some sort of product. People drive in off the expressway into daylit parking structures and find themselves in self-enclosed worlds disconnected to the rest of the city, ones designed to suck money up and out. Come to think of it, we're ahead of the curve on this as well. It's like another predatory economy, mortgage finance, which produces nothing but "phantom wealth," as David Korten calls it. And people do lose their homes and cars to both.

For the last decade the casinos have regularly been a stop on the Detroit Catholic Worker's Good Friday stations of the cross walk that names the powers and places where crucifixion is happening today.

> *"And they cast lots to divide his garments"* (Luke 23:34)
>
> ... Men in white shirts detail casinos on city maps, razing this or that old structure to lay a new cornerstone, imagining in their hearts a new foundation for Detroit's economy. In truth, this foundation is built upon sand. It would be constructed on nothing. Nothing but a lie, a conjurer's trick. Nothing but addiction and corruption. Nothing but a compulsive wish, a well-marketed false hope. No goods would be produced. No true services rendered. No spirit would be nourished. No neighborhood or community would be served.... And when the rains fall and the floods come and the winds beat against that house, not one stone will be left upon another.

GREENING THE AUTO POWERS?

Detroiters know that auto in large part created the American middle class. It built the city outward and out. And for some time we've seen coming the end of the line.

Last December when the initial auto industry loan was hanging in legislative balance and the US Big Three chiefs jetted into DC, a caravan of UAW workers drove from Detroit to Washington with a message: stop the union concessions being built into the plan; provide universal health care instead of building it into the cost of cars; *and* (notice this one) convert shuttered auto plants to production of mass transit and light rail vehicles, or even alternative energy equipment such as wind turbines. Now there's a worker vision.

Is this possible? I don't know anyone with blueprints, but the precedent most often cited (for good or ill) is Detroit as the Arsenal of

Democracy—when for three years during World War II industrial production in the city was quickly converted so that tanks, jeeps, and planes rather than cars rolled off the assembly lines of Detroit. To connect the plants with the airfields, the first expressways in the country were built (which, of course, in turn hastened the altering architecture of postwar urban landscape).

Presumably, such industrial greening would require a massive federal effort akin to a wartime mobilization. Now though, instead of war, on behalf of humanity and the planet. The times and reason are surely urgent enough. But beyond that, it would virtually require an act of repentance on the part of the auto companies. Theologically, it would entail a renewal of their corporate vocations to serve human life rather than growth (or now mere survival) let alone market share or even profit. Is that possible?

Remember it was the auto corporations who were aggressively complicit in the destruction of public transportation—such as paving over the street rail system in other cities, and encouraging the same in Detroit. It was they who joined in lobbying for the national fossil-fuel infrastructure of highways, *cul du sacs*, and sprawl, which we are even now tempted to renew. It was the American auto companies who found the way around emissions standards by inventing the SUV and manufacturing the desire for it through commercial advertising.

Greening auto jobs means more than planting grass on the roof of the Rouge Plant (yes, they have—and if not merely a public relations device, it's a good and necessary model for others). Greening means more, good though it be, than converting the Poletown plant (which three decades ago used eminent domain to level a Detroit neighborhood) from Cadillac production to GM's new electric car, the Volt. More than developing the big battery business in Michigan. It really means repenting the idolatry of the automobile. It means confessing that there's no going back, and we shouldn't even if we could. Can even the Angel of the Motor City face such a thing? Maybe.

BLOOM GREEN: RE-SPIRITING DETROIT FROM THE GROUND UP?

Kitty corner, across the street from my church, St. Peter's Episcopal, stand the remains of old Tiger Stadium. A new ball park named after a bank, and part of the run at casino economy, is located in the new sports and entertainment district closer to downtown. An attempt is ongoing to raise funds sufficient to save the historic field and club house for a museum and playing field. Given the times, I wouldn't bet on it. But I notice that the wound of demolition and removal of fully three-fourths of the old place is fresh enough that it still feels, every time I look, like a huge gaping hole has opened up in the world. That's Detroit. Things coming down and spaces opening up. But spaces mean possibility.

Thirty percent of Detroit is vacant land, nearly forty square miles in the city limits. Google Earth that! Last year three farms and over 200 school and community gardens bloomed in open spaces, plus nearly 400 family plots—and those are just the ones formally connected to Detroit's Garden Resource Network. Some of these are public school based, like Catherine Ferguson Academy, where pregnant teens and young mothers, in the shadow of the barn they themselves raised, each have an organic plot ringing the former football field (where horses now graze). Some are like the simple line of raised beds we constructed behind our church parking lot, a cooperative venture between congregants, neighbors, and soup kitchen participants. Some agricultural projects aren't properly gardens at all: picture an east side community planting 170 fruit trees throughout their neighborhood. And some gardens spring up on vacant land probably city owned, but who knows? It feels like no one's been in charge for a couple years, so people just seize the opportunity. But imagine if there actually were a programmatic city policy, with protected zoning for urban agriculture, or ways to legally get water from hydrants to vacant lots.

In fact the Detroit Black Community Food Security Network has shepherded through City Council a substantial resolution laying out policy directions related to food access, malnutrition, the role of schools and institutions, and urban agriculture. It's a beginning.

Do you know there's not a single brand-name grocery store left in the city of Detroit? The chains are gone. Neighborhood groceries remain, but the closest and easiest food sources tend to be dollar stores, gas stations, fast food outlets, and party stores. Too many people try to live on chips and pop. The United Food and Commercial Workers, who lost the union grocery jobs from the city, are facilitating conversations with community organizations about worker-owned stores that sell local food as a matter of policy. Perhaps more to the point, other conversations are in motion about a certified cannery where people could preserve and then sell their produce. A bigger operation could be making homegrown salsa, tomato sauce, and the like. Oh, bakeries of course—some amazing ones already, more planned. All feeding a budding system of small city farm markets.

Are these "green jobs"? Some of them are. And there would be more to speak of. (Including some stimulated by the green parts of the stimulus package.) But there's something of a shift going on among us from thinking about "jobs" (certainly those provided by corporations or government) to more entrepreneurial and community-based "work." In fact, some of them in gardening are more about community than jobs. They revive elder wisdom not yet lost and create intergenerational relationships. They foster real relationship to place and to earth and to the creatures even in the living soil. They reclaim neighborhoods as public communal spaces, safe ones. They encourage an economy of giving and sharing. An economy more of grace than consumption. We're actually talking about love and hope.

Currently there's a film making rapid rounds in Detroit. When I showed *The Power of Community: How Cuba Survived Peak Oil*, it was dropped off to me just in time by another pastor, and I had to return it elsewhere by midnight for university presentation the next day. Here's the story: when the Cold War ended, Cuba's oil spigot from the Eastern Bloc got shut off. Having once succumbed to petroleum-based, mechanized, Soviet-style agriculture, an island people, already under US embargo, had to figure out urgently how to survive without oil and feed themselves. Everybody lost twenty pounds. Bikes figured in, imported and newly produced. But above all organic and community-based gardening carried the day. They sprung up at first unbidden, by necessity, and then were supported by government policy. Today, half the food in Havana is grown in Havana! For smaller cities it's more like 80 percent. For the filmmakers it's an edifying lesson in how to survive the pending global collapse from the peaking of oil supplies. Me and a bunch of other Detroiters? We're thinking deindustrialization, and that Detroit could prove to be the Cuba of the rustbelt.

In some way Detroit's urban agriculture is a metaphor for a whole range of community-based creativity. Here's another: with 18 percent of Detroit homes vacant or abandoned, Tyree Guyton, now an internationally famed artist, turns a burned-out block of homes into a canvas for his artistic landscape, the Heidelberg Project. Cast-off appliances become found objects to be filled with other found objects. Vacuum cleaners line up like dominoes and wave their gloved hands at passers-by. Consumerism is mocked. Shopping carts hang upside down in the trees. Cars and car parts become something else altogether. Abandoned houses are covered with abandoned stuffed animals, or painted with polka dots, or glued with pennies. "God" and "war" are juxtaposed, brightly painted on TV screens or plywood sheets. It's a riot of color and ironic street imagination.

Detroit grows culture. Someday the poetry scene will be bound and published and digitalized, but for now you mostly gotta listen live, somewhere in the city every night. Musically, there was jazz and funk, Detroit rock, and, of course, Motown. Now the best of the hip-hop and performance artists aren't jockeying for major recording contracts, they are instead growing dozens of local labels in garages. Jenny Lee of the Allied Media Conference calls Detroit the Arsenal of Creativity. No wonder the United States Social Forum (Another World is Possible; Another US is Necessary) is bringing 15,000 activists to Detroit in the summer of 2010. It's the place to look and listen and learn.

It all makes me think. When the Hebrews walked out of slavery, out of Egypt, out of empire, they walked into the wilderness. That wilderness actually was itself the way out. The only way. The way out of no way. In the wilderness they had to unlearn a few things, namely slavery, Egypt, and empire. That lesson began with manna, the flaky food God provided. They had to learn what was gift sufficient and gather just enough for today. (What they over-gathered and hoarded stunk to high heaven.) They learned how to share and how to walk lightly upon the earth. In our own wilderness, on the way out of industrialism, we've got some things to learn and unlearn too. It seems like for Detroit and Detroiters, it begins with gathering what's on the ground.

2009

Reading Rivera: Remembering from Post-Industrial Detroit

THE RECORD (EPISCOPAL DIOCESE OF MICHIGAN)

Author's Note: This article has been edited in two ways. As it is a companion piece to the previous Resurrection City, material replicated in the former has been removed—which is to say, these must be read together and in one another's light. The review of Forgotten *is also pertinent to the Rouge Plant in this period. Secondly, I have given my theological and political tour of the murals many times now since. The insights of my guests have expanded my vision and in certain places I have likewise expanded my commentary.*

At the end of June 2010, upwards of 20,000 social justice activists are expected to gather in Detroit for the US Social Forum. They come here because *Another World is Possible; Another US is Necessary; and Another Detroit is Happening.* They come because Detroit already knows the economic devastation now faced in the rest of the country. They come because as survivors we know something about deindustrialization and how to live humanly in the midst of it, because we have a history of organizing, resistance, and community, and also because a new economy is being invented here from the ground up. Faith, spirituality, culture, and community are central to that re-creation.

No adequate visit to this beloved city is complete without a long slow meditation in the Rivera Court of the Detroit Institute of Arts. Diego Rivera, among the greatest Mexican artists of the last century, who composed these industrial murals depicting the Ford Rouge plant, is no mean theologian. Or so I would say. I myself, a white male pastor, am no academic theologian, never mind a student of art. But I do know what I love and I can tell you what I notice. And how I read it in a Detroit fast becoming the first postindustrial city.

Upon entering the cathedral-like space, the first thing one sees, high on the east wall, is an infant in a seed-womb planted deep in the earth. It seems to me a literalization of Psalm 139. *"For it was you who formed my inmost parts; you knit me together in my mother's womb.... My frame was not hidden from you when I was being made in secret, intricately woven in the depths of the earth"* (vv. 13, 15). Or perhaps the image from another angle in St. Paul: *"We know that the whole creation has been groaning in labor pains until now, and not only the creation, but we ourselves..."* (Rom 8:22). Placental veins and arteries on the wall reach as roots toward the Michigan fruits and vegetables grouped in panels and cradled in the arms of indigenous women. With first glimpse, we are on notice here: the topic is actually humanity in relation to creation. A birthing time and a holy enterprise as it were.

Below the child, and continuing around the room, are layers of earth —the elementals of car production: iron, coal, salt, limestone, sand.... In fact, earth is above, not below, in these murals, a kind of heavenly canopy —almost as though the plant, and even we ourselves as mural viewers, were inside the bulb, ready to sprout.

The religious structure is pretty explicit, combining the four directions of pre-Columbian spirituality with framing devices from European cathedrals in which Rivera studied. For example, the east wall of a cathedral —where the sun rises—is the creation wall. Think God and Adam touching in Michelangelo's portrayal. The west wall—where the sun sets—is the judgement wall where the sheep and the goats are separated on the last day. We shall come to that west wall.

The most notorious religious image, of course, is the controversial "nativity scene," which was one of several things that almost got the murals destroyed. An upper side panel on the medical industry portrays a child being vaccinated by a nurse-doctor couple, while the three wise scientists in the background develop the vaccine, and a cow, sheep, and horse gather in the fore. Insofar as the child, like the earth-wombed infant, represents all humanity, it is an early image for the possibility of universal health care as a human right. Today in Detroit, we might push the image further—beyond industrial medicine or insurance reform—to ask: what is wholeness and health? What is a healthy city or neighborhood? How is illness connected to injustice, or to corporate assaults of workplace, or addictive consumption, or toxic environment? How is personal health bound to human community? To a right relation with earth?

Another, less obvious, ecclesial form is most striking to me: along the base of the mural a dozen monochrome panels tell a kind of narrative sequence, a day in worker life, beginning with punching the clock and concluding with five workers trudging across a bridge to the gray sprawl of a parking lot. But something more liturgical is afoot. Rivera executed his work in eleven months, during 1932–33, at the height of the Great Depression. Seventy-five percent of the Rouge workforce was laid off and without public relief. In the winter of '32, just prior to his work, people were freezing and starving to death. On March 7 the Ford Hunger March was met on the Miller Street bridge by cops and company thugs with fire hoses and sub-machine guns. Five workers were killed and many more injured. Five workers on a bridge. These panels, in fact, reflect the traditional "stations of the cross."

Detroit community activist and lay minister Elena Herrada recalls her *abuelito* (as anti-church as Rivera himself) often saying, "Who wants to go to mass?" and then piling his grandchildren in the car for a reverential visitation to "our very own" murals. Her grandfather, Jose Santos Herrada, who had come from Mexico to work in the plants, would point to a brown-skinned figure on the north wall where the racial and cultural mix is notable, and say "That's me." Perhaps more to the point, in the period of its painting, he had been among the 15,000 people, including US citizens, from Detroit (and perhaps a million more across the country) "repatriated," forcibly and otherwise, to Mexico. Send home the immigrants stealing our jobs! A trail of tears in its own right, many died along the way. Among the many controversies of his work, Rivera donated certain of his profits to *los repatriados*, saying "Go back and start a cooperative in a land more hospitable."[3]

---

3. Balderrama and Rodriguez, *Decade of Betrayal: Mexican Repatriation in the 1930s*. Also, contact *Fronteras Nortenas* (http://www.losrepatriados.org), co-founded by Elena Herrada, to gather and protect the oral history of Detroit's *repatriado* community.

Today, at the end of auto, the union-breaking dismemberment of the industry has spun off a myriad of parts suppliers. And not just big ones like American Axle or Delphi bankrupting itself out of union contracts, but a host of smaller ones that function as *maquilladoras* of the north. In the Detroit area undocumented workers make fly wheels, seat covers, LCD screens, safety systems, and the like, for minimal wages and no benefits. In place of cops and company thugs, ICE (Immigration and Customs Enforcement) hovers ready to arrest and deport the wounded and malcontented. More stations on the trail.

Those who made the journey north to the industrial promised land (or north once again, as Herrada's grandfather in fact did) are portrayed in a line on that north wall. It is actually a prescient mix of immigrants who came in waves—eastern Europeans, Mexicans, American blacks and rednecks from the south, even Arabic peoples. It was the auto industry and the Rouge Plant that eventually drew and anchored in Detroit the largest Arabic community outside the Middle East. Rivera portrays them all working side by side in a common task. Would that it were yet fully so. Despite its black majority, Detroit has remained one of the more segregated urban areas of the nation. In point of fact, African American workers were for years separated off in the dirtiest, most dangerous and body-breaking jobs. They would, for example, be located largely in the foundry—insufferably hot. Insofar as Ford and the industrialists encouraged immigration it was partly to divide a gathering labor movement—pitting groups against one another culturally, linguistically, racially. (Ford, fiercely anti-union, didn't yield to unionization until wartime 1941.) But for Rivera, this mix, this rich human solidarity, as inclusive as the kin-dom of God or Martin King's "beloved community," held revolutionary hope and possibility.

With others, I was once treated to a guided tour of the murals by Pablo Davis, now of blessed memory, who as a young person assisted Rivera with their construction. Through a series of questions he pointed us to a vertical line that runs straight up the center of the north wall. From a base in that line of worker diversity, it begins in perhaps the mural's most famous image: those workers aligned in the back-breaking, hernia-straining task of moving engine blocks—and from there goes straight up through the fire of the smelting furnace, through some bundled sheaves, toward the volcano at the ceiling, dormant but ready to blow. The most brutal labor is the ignition spark in this revolutionary vision.

The biblical parallel to this is the "cry," the "groan" of the Hebrew slaves in Egypt. It goes up four times in two verses (Exod 2:23–24), straight up, as it were, to God, who hears and responds. It may be said that the groan beneath the imperial whip is what sets the whole biblical saga of liberation in motion. Before long they will be walking out from under empire into wilderness (which truly is the way out). The bush burns in the next chapter. The fire below and above is lit.

What if the history of suffering in Detroit is a spiritual resource waiting to be unleashed? A groan for the transformation of the city, even the nation? Here we say, our hope begins as grief.

Parallel and opposite the volcano, high on the south wall is a mountain made with hands—a pyramid. In fact there are great hands reaching out of the sun-browned structure in anger and anguish—one shakes a giant fist of resistance toward the placid figure of the "white" European, one of the archetypal "races" holding the four corners. Does the terraced mount signify for Rivera the conquered Mayan civilization, indeed the conquest of all first nations in the Americas? I say yes. But more. At a history deeper, and perhaps reading Rivera against Rivera, I'm inclined to think of biblical pyramids that always bespeak empire: towers of Babel, those Egyptian versions and granary towers built with Hebrew slave labor, Babylonian ziggurats. These skyscraping structures of power have their analogy in the Twin Towers or in Detroit's Renaissance Center. A pyramid itself is the very image of empire, of hierarchy resting on the backs of an enslaved base with a narrowing elite atop. Not a bad emblem for the whole industrial project, Fordist modernity.

Speaking of empire and looking west in the murals: one finds an early image of corporate globalization. Midlevel and center, a monochrome panel, which appears to be a sculpted limestone relief, portrays a river bearing along a freight ship. It is really two rivers meeting as one: the Detroit River and the greatest river on earth, the Amazon. It is their connection which speaks to industrial globalization.

Locally, the Detroit River basin defines the biological region in which we reside. The plants flushed their industrial machinery with the river. For the Rouge Plant the mainline to the Detroit River was in fact the River Rouge. Though a clean-up project has been hugely successful, in the sixties the Rouge was one of three rivers in the country to actually catch fire. Ironically, up stream it ran clear and clean through Fair Lane, the mansioned estate of Henry Ford, complete with a waterfall dam and a turbine system generating its own electricity. Thomas Edison sent a formal greeting to Ford for the dedication of the mansion's bird fountain. He wrote:

> *I am greatly pleased to do so because, while mankind appears to have been gradually drifting into an artificial life of merciless commercialism, there are still a few who have not been caught in the meshes of this frenzy and who are still human; and enjoy the wonderful panorama of the mountain, the valley, and the plain with their wonderful content of living things—and among those versions I am proud to know my two friends, John Burroughs and Henry Ford.*

About the scale of such self-delusions I have nothing to say.

Omitted from Rivera's image was the Ambassador Bridge, which had then recently been completed. Today, on the bridge Free Trade Agreements accelerate the truck traffic in commodities (and capital, of course, moves at the speed of light), though to human beings, Homeland Security tightens the gateway. The bridge's billionaire private owner now presses for a second span vying with the state against a downriver public version, while adjacent neighborhoods suffer his presumptions and the diesel fallout. The same neighborhoods are stalked by ICE and the Border Patrol. At our southern border the US build walls and the militarization is more complete.

In Rivera's portrayal the two great rivers are joined by a shipping route that connects the northern hemisphere with the global south. The left side of the panel is recognizable as Detroit by dockworkers, the skyline, and the powerboats accompanying the freighter. The South American side is represented by rubber workers, the trees having rubber extracted, and by giant fish swimming upstream. The workers, at different tasks, mirror each others' posture, suggesting their commonality and the hope of solidarity in a Pan-American union.

As should be clear, the murals are rich in ironies, subtle and blatant. Whether he knew it or not, this image of Rivera's would become increasingly so. Both ends reflect Ford Motor holdings at the time. Four years prior, in 1928, Ford had acquired two and half million acres along the Brazilian Amazon to grow his own rubber—at the time the only automobile raw material he did not control. But more, he tried to replicate there a Midwest American town, called Fordlandia, complete with hamburgers, a golf course, and telephone system. The indigenous trees (and their pests) resisted cultivation. And indigenous workers revolted against the cultural imposition of Americana, during one revolt smashing all the time clocks in the project. By 1945 the entire effort was abandoned and sold off without ever having delivered a single drop of latex to a Ford vehicle.[4]

Today market globalization assaults not only indigenous ways of life, but industrial ones. White flight figures into the devastation of Detroit, but no more than capital flight and deindustrialization. Unemployment in the city is almost 30 percent. In the last decade nearly a quarter-million auto-related jobs disappeared in the Metro area. They will not return.

The west wall does convey the separation of the judgement. Sheep and goats.

During World War II, Detroit plants were converted to war production: jeeps, tanks, and aircraft. The city became known as the Arsenal of Democracy. Rivera himself seems to foresee arsenalization. High on the west wall we look out, as through basement windows, toward the sky. On the left the civilian Ford tri-motor airplane is in production and on the right, its use as a fleet of warplanes with gas-masked airmen is envisioned. Follow further right to an adjacent panel on the north. In counterpoint to the healthcare nativity, eerie masked workers tend the construction of a poisonous gas bomb. It is practically tended as a "Little Boy." At the time of the painting these gas bombs had already been rendered illegal under international law, but the painter sees them being made. The gas weaponry of World War I, along with aerial bombardment, had ruptured the pretense of moral boundaries, opening the wide door to anti-personnel devices and weapons of mass destruction. The panel summons to mind the weapons used now in Iraq, Afghanistan, and Gaza—not to mention the undergirding nuclear arsenals of the US and others.

The industrialist himself is situated in the war corner. On the lower right west wall a composite of Henry Ford and Thomas Edison spreads out his own blueprint. Above him a hawk scattering doves is the emblem. It's worth noting that in the thirties, the auto companies were investing in what came to be the Axis powers. Ford's plants in Germany were never bombed. Another early wave of corporate globalization. Ford was actually enamored of Adolf Hitler and if Germany had won the war, he would have come out impeccably Nazi, I suppose.

---

4. Grandin, *Fordlandia: The Rise and Fall of Henry Ford's Forgotten Jungle City*. See also *The Amazon Awakens*, a documentary on Fordlandia produced in 1944 by Walt Disney for the US Coordinator of Inter-American Affairs.

My wife Denise first pointed out to me that the dynamo generator behind him forms an industrial-sized ear. This is telling as well. Henry Ford was notorious for his surveillance.[5] Even of the murals themselves. Each night he would have Rivera's work photographed and pictures brought to him for study. Apparently, Rivera was too deft or Ford too artistically challenged to get the bitter ironies and critical vision. The risks to the piece were real. Rivera's next project in New York City was in fact destroyed by Nelson Rockefeller, his erstwhile benefactor.[6]

Ford's ear on the shop floor is represented on the south wall, a lower left panel of the final assembly where a foreman surveying the scene seems to eye the viewer suspiciously. (He is one of only five figures who stare out of the mural directly at us.) More than one Rouge manager has been suggested for the portrait. Bricker is one. I myself always imagined him Harry Bennett, Ford's enforcer and then heir apparent. If so I further imagine a .38 concealed by his coat. Of note here is that in the thirties there was one supervisor for every seven workers. Rivera has painted only one supervisor in the whole plant. Here in his vision, the workers run the means of production.

On the left side of the west wall at our level is a worker. He wears gloves with red stars on them and a heavy hammer in is hand. Fact is, there was actually such a thing as Red Star Gloves. Rivera has cleverly juxtaposed them with the hammer as a suggestive political reference to communism.

There is a similar juxtaposition in the south wall. Center left there is a worker wearing a hat that says "We want." Again this is an accurate contemporary representation. During prohibition in the thirties some wore hats that proclaimed, "We want beer." Rivera has made the word beer invisible and in its place painted, yes, another hammer in motion.

Above him a crowd of visitors on tour looks on it seems in disapproval. They are a conspicuously religious crowd, including a priest and two pious Bible-toting church ladies with scowls. The priest makes one

---

5. I forebear to open the topic of political surveillance here. It has become omni-competent. NSA, FBI, CIA, Homeland Security. However, it is commercial surveillance that has become numbingly ubiquitous. Not simply shop-floor cameras, but those in malls, and stores, and building-mounted on street corners. Add the consolidation of credit card data collection, shopping cards, cookies and computer spyware, Facebook, and the like.

6. Not Henry Ford, but Edsel was the benefactor of the mural. To suppress or destroy it, father would have had to go through son. Rivera's refusal to compromise his vision and the resulting destruction of the New York mural is portrayed in two popular films: *Frida* and *Cradle Will Rock*.

think of Father Coughlin, a Ford confidant with his own radio show, also pro-fascist, presaging the era of hate radio. Rivera would be woefully aware of him.

When Pablo Davis gave us his tour, he asked, "Do you see any cars in the mural?" We hunted the twisting motion of the line and its rich human narrative. Nary a one. Then he lifts his cane to point it out: dead center on the south wall, about two inches big at the vanishing point of the perspective. Represented here was the precise opposite of what Marx called commodity fetishization, where human value is projected onto a thing, inflating it in scale and import and summoning it into a life of its own. In a great inversion, commodities become personified and persons become commodified. Rivera's reduction to a point, withdrawing the projection, likewise marked the opposite of what the biblical texts call idolatry or that which they name as a "principality." This is the very idolatry that has been writ large in consumerism. If Henry Ford had painted the mural (never mind had he understood it), the car would have been huge as an SUV billboard, and the human beings miniscule cogs on the line.

There is a confirmation of this analysis in the mural itself. Down left from there, in one of the monochrome panels, Henry Ford himself teaches a class of workers. Before him is an engine mounted on feet much like a dog's. Another look shows the timing pullies to be a face and the gearshift to be a wagging tail—the engine has indeed come alive. Behind Ford two rows of people bend over a long table—reading blueprints? Their hands are outstretched before them and their heads bowed as if in worship. The table disappears into the vanishing point—where Ford's teaching finger precisely points and rests. As if to say "Look to the vanishing point of the mural." A little tutorial in commodity fetishization.

I believe when Rivera began to sketch the first cartoons designing the mural, it was more blocked and boxy. But when the assembly line commended itself, suddenly the unity of the entire thing in motion took shape. Once I was with a friend from L.A. surveying the murals. He said, "You know, this is the period when motion pictures were coming into their own. The line looks like film threading through the scenes." Next time I gave a little tour I repeated his line and someone said, "Look, there's the camera or projector!" Sure enough, the big machinery on the left looks just so.

Diego Rivera's industrial vision in the murals is substantially positive. At a time when economic collapse had the Rouge 70 percent laid off, he portrays a worker-run, racially and culturally diverse work force going full tilt. Industrialization in the hands of workers. Read from the present postindustrial landscape, of capital flight, industrial flight, job flight, white flight . . . we are in dire straits and perhaps extreme opportunity.

Of the five or six mural characters who look out at us, directly into our own eyes, there is the laconic museum curator in the lower right south beside Edsel holding the benefactor's commission, there is Harry Bennet (drawing a bead and targeting us all), there is the androgynous Asian looking down impassively from a rising sand economy, there is the cryptic little gas-masked character peeking out of western judgement far right west, there is the Christ child in the medical nativity with his halo and that stern stark stare, and then there is Diego Rivera himself, upper left on the north wall—green-faced in a bowler, hiding in the gas-ridden toxic corner, eyeing us as with a great question.

2010

Station: Chase Bank—The Financial Industry

Then one of the twelve, called Judas Iscariot, went to the chief priests and said, "What are you willing to give me if I deliver him to you?" And they counted out to him thirty pieces of silver. So from that time he sought opportunity to betray him. (Matt 26:14–16)

Recently, a delegation of African American pastors to the tobacco fields of North Carolina were shocked at the circumstances in which undocumented workers labor. They said, these are the same fields in which our ancestors toiled as slaves, and the conditions are virtually unchanged. When FLOC (the Farm Labor Organizing Committee) began to follow the economic chain upward, they went through small farmers to the Farm Bureau Federation to RJ Reynolds to major investments by Chase Bank.

Chase drives the nail.

The taxpayer bailout of US banks is now approaching a trillion dollars. JP Morgan Chase is the second largest bank in the United States. With Wells Fargo and Bank of America, it is among those foreclosing on Detroiters, profiting from their loss. From bailout dollars, fees and processing, foreclosure insurance paid by homeowners, and varieties of bundling, Chase makes more on foreclosures than on mortgages. In fact, by legislation and funding, the five largest banks hold 3.3 million mortgages eligible for modification, but have only modified 30,000. Estimates anticipate 326,000 more foreclosures in Michigan by 2012.

Chase and the others drive the nail.

There is more to be made. Chase is on the board of Living Cities, the source for Mayor Bing's downsizing plan, clearing entire neighborhoods. Urban removal from above. More dislocations. And a trail of tears. Who drives the nail?

Verse: *Were you there when they stole my life and home?*

2011

Station: Official Violence and Restorative Justice

Holy Trinity School—Site of a Beating

"For Christ is our peace; in his flesh he has abolished the dividing wall of hostility between us . . . that he might create in himself one new humanity in place of the two, thus making peace, and might reconcile both groups to God in one body through the cross, thus putting to death that hostility through it." (Eph 2: 14–16)

Last October as Charlie Duncan, a street resident of Corktown and a regular at Manna Community Meal, was bedding down for the night in the alcove of this school, he was first threatened then attacked with a baseball bat by another Corktown resident. This violence and hostility reflect a pattern of informal and official harassment of homeless folks in our neighborhood. They functions as the blunt end of pending development, toward the urban removal of poor people.

Many in the neighborhood have responded to this incident. A restorative justice committee has formed, asking: who all was wounded in this act? Who all is responsible? How can the divide of hostility be broken down? What are the remedies and reparations possible? How can street people be counted here as citizens and full members of the community?

Two years ago on Good Friday in Northeast Detroit, Robert "Tazzy" Mitchell, a teenager with a learning disability, was in a car stopped by Warren police on Eight Mile Road (the dividing wall of hostility within

Detroit). Panicking, Robert fled, was chased into an abandoned house, and there, in capture, was killed with an electroshock taser by police.

Many in the city, including his mother Cora Renee Mitchell and the Coalition Against Police Brutality, not only demanded justice and an end to taser use, but have called for "Peace Zones for Life"—in this case reaching both deep into the community and across its boundaries in the work of peace-building. At the foot of the cross this work is going forward. Christ's wounded body is transformed into a peace zone in this world—it becomes the beloved unity of a new humanity.

Verse: *Were you there when the poor were struck and died?*

2012

Station: Trayvon Martin and Young Black Males

CLEM KERN STATUE

Then the soldiers, when they had crucified Jesus, took His garments and made four parts, one share for each soldier, and also the tunic [the long shirtlike undergarment]. But the tunic was seamless, woven in one piece from the top throughout. So they said to one another, "Let us not tear it, but let us cast lots to decide whose it shall be." (John 19:23–24)

Seventeen-year-old Trayvon Martin was fatally shot February 26 by a neighborhood watch volunteer in the gated community of Sandor, Florida. He wore a hoodie against a light rain. He was followed as he left the store headed back to the home of his father's fiancé. The shooter has not been arrested or charged, claiming self-defense under Florida's "stand your ground" law.

Since 2006 Michigan has had a similar law permitting "no retreat" and allowing the use of deadly force if a person claims to feel threatened with bodily harm.

But the fact is: young black males are the ones threatened and profiled and targeted in our society. They are criminalized in the school to prison pipeline. (Information leaked to the press by Florida police about Martin included the fact that he had been suspended from school). One in three black males in their twenties are in prison or under the control of correctional supervision. They are cast as predators and so as juveniles given mandatory life sentences. In Detroit they are seven times more likely to die of violence than young white males. Here in a city where the unemployment rate runs 20–25 percent, for young African Americans it is upwards of 60 percent. Young black men are scapegoats in a society of fear and violence.

Supporters of justice in the case have claimed the hoodie and taken to wearing it as an act of solidarity. Jesus the Crucified joins that intercession, saying "I am Trayvon Martin."

Verse: *Were you there when they targeted the young?*

2012

Place-Based Communities of Faith: Questions Toward the Beloved Neighborhood

Detroit Reader, James and Grace Lee Boggs Center to Nurture Community Leadership, 2012.

GIVING THE LOCAL PRIDE OF PLACE

The rise, dominance, and temporary victory of the global market, has entailed an assault on all things local—governance, culture, habitat, and above all, community. Movements of resistance (witness the Zappatistas in Chiapas as a prime example) have increasingly organized around the renewal of the local, honoring the concrete sacredness of place.

In Detroit the experiments take many forms. Think of place-based governance (the renewal and practice of participatory democracy in resistance to external emergency managements), place-based peacemaking and security through peace zones and neighborhood restorative justice, place-based social media where neighborhoods connect and link by wireless or even pirate radio, place-based education (is it possible to envision genuinely rooted neighborhood schools when public education is dismantled by design and Detroit schools are forced into a statewide failing school district?), place-based art that murals local history, the re-rooting of food production in the community, rebuilding the latter through the urban gardening movement, and of course the relocalization of economy in place-based economic forms, from local currencies and time-banks to co-ops, CSR's, and community entrepreneurism. All of these emphasize relationship—to one another in the neighborhood, to a living environment, and to earth itself.

Little wonder that the idea of place-based churches and communities of faith would be put forward. As with the others this sounds like a new idea, but it's actually an ancient one in a new moment and context. In certain traditions a place-based church is what used to be called a parish: the turf or territory for which a congregation intercedes and takes spiritual responsibility. (In Louisiana, parishes morphed into geographic units of local governance.)

In one churchly tradition, for example, parish boundaries were defined by how far a liturgical procession could walk to bless the fields on "Rogation Sunday." Notice this combination of elements: a human unit of scale encompassing community based on walking distance, a connection to earth (the rootedness in planting and harvest), and the blessings of prayer. Not a bad mix. Plumb the meaning of an apparent spiritual anachronism: Think of orthodox Jews in their odd and prayerful commitment to walking to temple on Shabbat.

In the book of Jeremiah, the prophet writes a letter to the exiles, the "resident aliens," the strangers within empire, captive in Babylon. He urges them to seek the shalom of the place in which they reside, for in its shalom their own would be found. Build, he says, and plant, marry and have children. Put down roots in that place. The Hebrew notion of shalom (kin to Arabic *salaam*) is far more than either peace or justice, it is the two as one, woven in relationship. Shalom is wholeness that is right relation to God, to one another in community, to the earth and all creation. By the way, the Greek word for "resident aliens," *parachoi*, is also the root word under parish. A further note, one of caution: This is also root of "parochial"—with all its in-turned and narrow, even xenophobic, dangers inherent. The love of the local, the focus on place, must not mean ignorance or blindness, either to stranger or the global—but in fact the very way into them. We can still think globally while living and loving locally.

DETROIT DISS-LOCATION AND FAITH COMMUNITY

Social psychiatrist Mindy Fullilove speaks of "root shock," as the personal and social disorientation brought on by the destruction of a community's emotional ecosystem. Her book by that name[7] details a history of Urban Renewal (Negro removal) which, in the midst of the Freedom Struggle, structurally assaulted the rooted places from which the African American community drew its life. She describes an archipelago of urban ghettos where music, culture, and meaning thrived, all of which were destroyed first with contagious housing destruction, and then with the blunt end of the bulldozer. She includes a short story by her father recounting his intuitive wisdom of place—an evening of culture and conversation with Homeboy in Detroit's Paradise Valley and the Black Bottom neighborhood, now long gone to removal.

In 1980 the City of Detroit set out to clear a near east side neighborhood for General Motors to build a Cadillac plant. This was not the first time the power of eminent domain was used to clear or break up an entire neighborhood (think: Black Bottom or Mexican Town), but it was its first ever use on behalf of a profit-making corporation. And first against a diverse, but European-majority neighborhood. Here was a community with deep labor history in the sit-down strikes of the thirties, and they prepared to fight for their homes and neighborhood. Immaculate Conception Church became the locus of the resistance. After the neighborhood organization won a temporary victory in court, the archdiocese sold the church out from under them and evicted the priest. It was a dispiriting and decisive event that officially subverted the community's struggle. Within a year the neighborhood was reduced to a 465-acre site of empty land suitable for redevelopment. Believe it or not, there was a cemetery in the neighborhood that could not be moved. The story is that it is still on the grounds, and is opened twice a year for two-hour visitations. Though General Motors wished to erase altogether the memory of the former community, even naming the main entry road, "Lucky Place," people still refer to the Detroit/Hamtramck Facility as the "Poletown" Plant.

As the city's population continued to decline, this church closing proved the first in several waves of such. They were all essentially high-handed top-down decision processes of closing by announcement. A year or so ago, the Archdiocese of Detroit was preparing to name another round of churches to be closed. Before finalizing decisions, however, the cardinal met with Mayor Bing. Although there was yet no "plan" for the downsizing of the city, it was becoming progressively clear that certain neighborhoods were slated for resources and development while others would see services

---

7. Fullilove, *Root Shock*.

progressively withdrawn and infrastructure untended. Now in addition to the withdrawal of police, fire, and sanitation services, along with the boarding up of schools, churches would coordinate their closings as well. Neighbors who had not yet been foreclosed upon would be fending for themselves in maintaining any semblance of community. There are ways the church can join in the disassembling of place.

In the mainline Protestantism of Detroit, the delocalization of the church has been substantially connected to white flight. As Europeans moved to the suburbs certain congregations would move wholesale and quickly, buying a tract of land and building a new church in a developing area. (There was, to be sure, a Jewish equivalent of this process.) Other congregations moved slowly toward dissolution. Parishioners continued to drive back for a time to their former churches. They kept political control of the building and congregational life as it became increasingly a commuter church and then dwindled into demise. Both these tactics disconnected the church (rapidly or by degrees) from the city neighborhood as space for ministry and accountability. Place was abandoned and dishonored.

Ironically, this disconnection cycled forward spiritually. African American churches (Pentecostal, Apostolic, Baptist, Independent) were growing in this same period. Empty, formerly white churches were on the market at fire-sale prices. Black congregations would find a building suitable to their needs and purchase. Congregants drove to the new location for services, but these too were "commuter churches." The connection to the neighborhood was essentially concerned with conflicts over street parking on Sunday morning. Sometimes they would grow further and move on to a new and larger facility elsewhere. The relationship of the church to place was essentially severed.

LOCATION, LOCATION, LOCATION: REIMAGINING PLACE-BASED CONGREGATIONS

An obvious first consideration toward the renewal of place: where do the leaders, clerics, pastors, and above all congregants live in relation to the "parish"? Walking distance? Even biking? Among the principles of the Christian Community Development Association are "Reconciliation, Redevelopment, and Relocation."[8] Sometimes the latter has meant white folks moving wholesale (and perhaps naively) into communities of color, but the

---

8. From the wide body of literature on CCDA I suggest Gornik, *To Live in Peace*.

principle of living in the neighborhood in which one builds community and ministry is pretty significant, often ignored, and almost always decisive.

To be sure, congregations seeking to live the Beloved Community take many forms. Those consciously rooted in place will take unique approaches to their context. A metropolitan congregation will appear as a commuter community drawing members from far and wide, yet may deliberately attend the vocation of an entire city. Churches may form organizational and interfaith alliances to intercede for a wider, though still discrete, urban turf. (In *The Death and Life of Great American Cities*, Jane Jacobs identifies three types of "neighborhoods": the street-level neighborhood, the district, and the city as a whole, each of which might be thought of as urban places.)

What then would be the issues and elements for the renewal of a congregation in place-based ministry?

Let's start unlikely and logically. What if the congregation vocationally tended, sought, and helped keep the deep memory of place? What if worshipers even knew geology and the watershed, the rock and river, the streambeds buried beneath the streets?

In Detroit the remaining tract of original terrain is fittingly a cemetery, Elmwood/Mt. Elliot, bounded by a Baptist church and a Capuchin monastery. What if faith-folk recognized indigenous plants like chicory and wild carrot (so-called Queen Anne's Lace), and noticed them creeping up between cracks of concrete? Can we defend this space from environmental assault? Can we protect the river or the trees (not to mention the health of the community abiding here) from the contempt of pollution and degradation?

What if we honored the first people to camp here, to call it home? To name it like they name themselves. In Detroit the Ojibwa called this *Wawiatonong*, "where the river goes round." The shore was for them a place of meeting. And they trod lightly upon its banks. The French called it *de troit*, "the straits." They built the first church. It was for them a place of trading and eventually of forts that were held and fought for with warships. Europeans made of the river a border between nation-states. The industrial powers saw in it a source of transportation: furs and ores and manufactured goods. With it they washed their machines, flushing away petrochemicals and waste. Who remembers and who forgets the storied history of this place?

Which is to say, who is buried here? In the early centuries of the Christian church it was not that remains of the martyrs and saints that were placed in the altar as a vault to sanctify the space. Exactly the opposite. Pilgrims came to the holy place of burial and the church grew up around it almost like a shelter. The grave became the table for a feast day, an *offrenda*, beloved bones invoking the memory beneath.

Does your congregation know the human waves of resident aliens and immigrants inhabiting your place? What were the movements, the struggles for space, for dignity, for justice that went down? Who here were the prophets, the local ancestors? Who planted and who built? Who were the martyrs, the unsung, the heroes notorious? And who are the elders yet living who know the stories, the graves, that very movement landscape? Who is recording their oral history and honoring them publicly? Who is painting the mural that tells the tale? Is this a churchly errand or not?

So often these days, young folks come to the post-industrial city "to make it livable again." They bear a refrain that here is a "blank slate," an "empty canvas" on which to ply their urban dreams and schemes. The mix of good intention, privilege, and presumption is essentially blind to the layered meanings of place. Imposing a narrative of their own construction, they come as protagonists without ken of blood and earth beneath the street or the presence of living community and its struggle. As they say, you can't really grow a place you don't fully love. You can't really love a place you don't truly know.

As with the art of entrepreneurialism, does knowing and remembering actually bear on ministry in this place? Well, ask this then, what is the story of your own community of faith, even your building, and how does it connect to or root in all that's gone before? Put it as discernment: how has God been, is God now, present in this place through your community? More to the point, where do you as a community recognize God alive and at work in this place and join your hand to the presence?

For over three decades my faith community in near southwest Detroit has undertaken an annual liturgical event, to publicly walk the "stations of the cross" on Good Friday.[9] Drawing on traditional ritual it remembers the execution of Jesus in the here and now. Lent, the season leading up to it, becomes a time of discernment to recognize both where Christ is being crucified today and where ministries of love and justice respond. We carry

---

9. Wylie-Kellermann, *Seasons of Faith and Conscience*, xxv, 1, 18, 20, 110. The stations were originally a place-specific liturgy, walking the *via dolorosa* through the streets of Jerusalem. Transposed to a "universal" litany of historical memory in churches and cathedrals, our practice in Detroit re-localizes the liturgy around current sites of suffering "on the ground."

a cross through the neighborhood and downtown. We stop for meditation and prayer at specific sites. Each year the landscape we walk has changed to one degree or another. Ground shifts beneath our feet. Spaces open and fill with new cries. Buildings disappear or spring up before us. The faces of victims and executioners rise up to us from a particular historical moment, in a particular place, both our own.

Several notes on this "liturgy of place": First is the matter of walking, on which we have already touched. Here again, prayer is afoot, a walking meditation, a moving contemplative practice. What if every time the congregation delivered its newsletter door to door, stoop to stoop, the eyes of the heart were wide open? What if the rabbi or imam or pastor weekly walked the streets of the neighborhood in search of conversation and street-level news? Even in clerical garb. Some years ago Rev. B. Herbert Martin of Chicago's south side used to walk among the gang-homed projects bearing his shepherd's crook as a walking stick. His was a well-known and accessible presence.

Second, is the issue of the powers-that-be. To know a place is also to recognize its occupation by empire. Where do the structures of power (corporations, institutions, government agencies, developers, polluters, major non-profits, foundations, etc.) have a foot on the ground in the neighborhood? Where do they stake a claim? Where to their smoke stacks rise? Reading the landscape of place means mapping these powers with open eyes as well. And it may mean confronting, rebuking, and telling them the truth for the sake of those on the ground.

Related: turf-based organizing (Alinsky and his kin) has historically focused on needs and deficits in the community—from whence does the suffering cry rise? This is not beside the point. A congregation which has stopped its ears to the groans from the ground will not discern potential ministries and work set before it.

THE BELOVED NEIGHBORHOOD

On the other hand, I have come in recent years to wonder if we shouldn't also be celebrating on foot the "stations of resurrection" as well. Where on our streets is life breaking out irrepressibly? What are the signs of resurrected community? How is humanity being renewed and restored?

In counter-response to the need-based approach, this is more in accord with the "asset-based community development." Here it is the resources of the community, the gifts on the ground (personal, institutional, elements of earth or the built environment, spaces open or public) that are identified and mapped.

A faith community can survey its turf for these assets and imagine a new ensemble of possibilities. Notice, appreciate, and connect them in relationship. It's just as easy to be blind to the resources of community hidden in plain sight, right before our eyes. Where new and creative initiatives—in economy or social organizing—are happening, these can be supported, nourished, encouraged.

In Detroit, The Coalition Against Police Brutality, so proficient at researching and calling out police violence, has now taken to advocating as well Peace Zones for Life. They hold out a vision of neighborhood security based on community responsibility for violence and conflict. "Peace zone" or "shalom zone" is not a bad synonym for "parish." What if peace congregations took responsibility for their neighborhoods in exactly this way? At St. Peter's we are working to open a neighborhood center for restorative justice, where violence, conflict, and crime can be addressed by the community. Where we can circle to ask, who has been, or is being, harmed? Who is responsible? And what remedies can we name and covenant together toward justice and wholeness? At present in our neighborhood, many of these questions fall along a fault line between neighborhood residents, old and new, and street folk who have a long-standing "home" in this place. It all comes down to: how can we live humanly and justly together?

Some of this work is ephemeral, fragile as breath. Given the graves, given the stories that haunt, given the cultural memories shared and life ripening, a neighborhood has a palpable spirit, an ethos, an "angel of the place" if you will. A rooted congregation will discern that spirit, honor it, bless and nourish it. The Canadian troubadour and poet Joni Mitchell used to tune her guitar to the sounds and harmonics of the place for which she would write a song. Place-based congregations might do much the same.

EXPULSION SUITE

2013

We Shall Not Be Moved:
Words Won't Make it Happen

SECRET SOCIETY OF TWISTED STORYTELLERS, MARCH 21, 2014—CHARLES WRIGHT MUSEUM OF AFRICAN AMERICAN HISTORY, DETROIT

Good evening. Thank you to Satori Shakour and to all the storytellers of the evening.

The last time that I tried to cross into Canada I was stopped at the border. After a few questions I was sent to a waiting area, and the wait was long. Eventually a woman came to the Plexiglas window and she had one of those thick folded computer printouts. "Have you ever been arrested?" she said. "Yeah." She leaned forward and said, "Tell me about depredation of property in Alexandria Virginia in 1979." " I'm pretty sure it was the anniversary of the bombing of Hiroshima, and we poured blood on the pillars of the Pentagon and used our bodies to lock the doors shut as a protest against US nuclear policy."

She looked down the list, shaking her head. I knew it was my rap sheet, but more what I'd actually like to think of as a history of conscience. I wondered what all was there. I knew it was not just the Pentagon but there could be the White House, the Capitol, assorted SAC bases, missile factories, the federal buildings here in Detroit, and the Detroit Economic Club. One time I was arrested for dumpster-diving food for a soup kitchen in Grand Rapids. And I actually fell in love with my wife Jeannie when we were handcuffed together repeatedly, coming and going from the Oakland County jail. We were charged with contempt and conspiracy under the prosecutorial regime of L. Brooks Patterson in those days.

My first arrest was as a seminarian in New York City, at a Columbia University military think tank. I had fallen under the sway of Daniel Berrigan. Berrigan is a Jesuit priest, a poet, a prophet of nonviolence. And he came to teach at the seminary fresh from two years in federal prison for burning draft files in Catonsville, Maryland as a protest against the war in Southeast Asia. Berrigan knocked me off my horse. Here I was, raised in the church, already in seminary, and suddenly I'm going through a conversion to the gospel. It was his life of course, but concretely the way that he read Scripture, not just as a poet, though that for sure, but as if it was a matter of life and death. He followed a Jesus who was executed for resistance to the official violence of occupation and empire, and now I was following too.

Actually I think the seed of this call went back further. Because one time rummaging through my attic I stumbled on my high school term paper, where you learned in those days to use note cards. And my paper was on civil disobedience. I was actually shocked to remember it. So I was early on influenced by Gandhi, and Thoreau, but especially Martin Luther King's "Letter from a Birmingham Jail," where he explains the importance of direct action and civil disobedience in the Freedom Struggle.

I graduated from Cooley High School in 1967. I know that King's letter affected how I saw the smoke rising from Twelfth Street corridor that summer, the fires of the Detroit Rebellion. There's a passage, I won't quote it accurately, but Dr. King is accused of bringing violence to Birmingham and he says "we didn't bring violence to Birmingham, violence was here. We just brought it into the open, into the light of day."

Perhaps you know that last year was the fiftieth anniversary of that letter, and on the very date, April 16, the Detroit City Council voted on the Jones Day contract. Now, Jones Day, as I trust you are aware, is the third largest law firm in the world with their main clients being the very banks that have eaten the substance out of our neighborhoods with predatory mortgages. Yes, the same banks who have made predatory loans to the city of Detroit, the so-called Swaps and Cops. It's the law firm partnered by Emergency Manager Kevyn Orr. As of this week, Detroit's been under emergency management for one year. Can you believe that virtually every African American city in the state of Michigan, half the state's African American population, live under non-elected governments? Three quarters of our black elected officials have been replaced by emergency managers.

So when the Jones Day contract came up for a vote before City Council, I kind of knew this was an important moment. A group of us, mostly young people actually, went to City Council that morning. We spoke during the public comment period. My own comments concerned the anniversary of the letter and how it's addressed to white pastors. Dr. King expresses great disappointment at the tepid passivity of white pastors in the Freedom Struggle and, to be honest, that had laid a claim on me.

So, when the moment came for the vote, this whole group of us knelt down in the aisle and we began to sing, "We shall not, we shall not be moved. We shall not, we shall not be moved. Just like a tree that's planted by the water, we shall not be moved." When we did that, several things happened. One was that it seemed to release, and free the whole crowd who was there, maybe sixty or eighty people, present to speak on this issue and others. They all rose up simultaneously and started addressing the council directly. To be frank, there was a lot of anger in the room. I remember one man pounding his hand on the rail in front of the council area. There was a Korean War veteran who pleaded with the council, saying "I fought for this country for four years and now they're going to take my house away in foreclosure." Lots of anger and chaos. So we would sing slowly and loudly trying to bring the focus back down. One woman, gorgeously dressed with this wide-brimmed Sunday morning hat, was there to talk about her mother's water bill. She came and stood with us; she had the voice of an angel and when she joined us, suddenly we sounded like we a choir, with harmony and rhythm.

Well, we expected that we would be arrested pretty quickly, but in fact we sang for an hour and a half. We could see the police arrive. Actually, officers came pretty quickly, visible through the glass doors. They had handcuffs ready to go. Most of the council had left the room and some of them appeared with the police, clearly urging arrest. On the other hand there were two council members, Councilwomen JoAnn Watson and Brenda Jones, who stayed right in their seats. I believe they remained to witness what was happening and receive it, but also to protect us with their presence. So the police were put in this conflict, first of all in themselves. On the one hand they were under orders, and on the other, it was their pensions put up for grabs at the hands of Jones Day. And they knew that; they knew that.

Something else happened that I've never experienced before: someone I know a little bit began whispering in my ear. "Reverend, you've done what you came to do. It's, you know, time to stop." And I said, "No, we're not stopping." And he came back a minute later, the voice whispering in my ear urging "Reverend Charles Williams," who I do know, and trust, and work with, "he wants you to stop, he thinks you should stop." I doubted that was true, but I said "We're not stoppin'." And the voice came one more time, saying "Look, we have the votes to prevent this thing; we need to let them vote." That proved not to be true. And it was also an untruth that was now being spread through the crowd. I confess I've had voices like that in my own head before. You know, don't do this, or you've taken it far enough; you know, back off, step back. But I've never had this literal whispering in my ear. I think about how the media in Detroit are whispering all the time in our ears saying "This is just the way it is, and there's nothing you can do about it. Stand down."

Well, eventually, when the officers did come in, the woman with the broad Sunday cap, bless her soul, she was with us ready to go—she held out her hands to be cuffed. So did the Korean War vet offer himself as part of this. But in the end only two of us were arrested: myself and Elena Herrada, a member of the elected Detroit School Board, a warrior in the struggle for children and justice in the city. We were handcuffed, and taken through the crowd, down the elevator, to Jefferson where a big blue police bus waited. And immediately, we went to the back of the bus, thinking, "Oh, there are going to be more waves of arrests and this thing is going to fill up." But no. It wasn't long and the bus pulled out. We had the entire thing to ourselves going to the precinct, where we were congenially processed. And I should say that when we were released into our own recognizance that the police officers thanked us, and one even embraced us.

In the months that followed we had a number of times in the thirty-sixth district court. At the arraignment we requested a jury trial. And the judge said "Why do you want a jury trial for petty misdemeanor?" and we answered "Because under emergency management, a jury is the last vestige of democracy in the city of Detroit." And that's true. We were defending ourselves; we didn't want lawyers. The judge and the prosecutor, and any number of people would repeatedly say to us when we told we were defending ourselves—they would quote the adage, "a lawyer who would defend him or herself had a fool for a client." The implication, of course, was that we had fools for lawyers. But we knew that we would be able to speak more freely, and we wanted to put ourselves on the stand. Our idea was to put Jones Day on trial. And we were set with a number of witnesses, including the honorable JoAnn Watson, prepared to testify who could say she was there and could testify to what happened; but she would also be an expert witness on the state of Detroit, on the conflict of interest involved, and the legal malfeasance implied in the contract. On the day of the trial, I was all prepared with what I would say to the jury in my closing statement. And of course juries are instructed: you can consider this but you can't consider this, you know. And of course what they can't consider is conscience, their conscience and ours, the context for action and what's going on in the city. I was trying to think of how I could let them know the power that they actually have. Because in the end they just say "guilty" or "not guilty." They have way more power than they're allowed to know. And that's what it comes down to being that last vestige of democracy.

Well, on the morning of the trial, the police officers didn't show up. And they were the prosecution's whole case. I don't know, was it the weather, the polar vortex? Did they make a decision; did they think they were giving us a gift? In any event, by their not being present the judge dismissed the charges against us, and we never got to say what we did or why we did it, which I suppose, is why I'm telling you. Maybe story listeners are the last vestige of democracy in Detroit.

["Not guilty!"—from the audience]

Conscience prevails.

Next week, I'm going to New York City just for a day or two, I want to see Daniel Berrigan. He's ninety-three. His mind is really sharp but his body is quite frail. I want to thank him, not only for the fifty-some books he's written that've moved my soul, but for the quality of his life and his witness of action over and over and over. Maybe I'll end with a poem of his. He's a brilliant poet. So this is something short:

> For every 10,000 words
> there's a deed
> floating somewhere
> head down, unborn

Words can't make it happen
They only wave it away
unwanted.
Yet Child, necessary one
Unless you come home to my hands
Why hands at all?
Your season your cries
are their skill
their reason.

Thank you.

2013

Statements of the Accused: No Consent. Go on Record. Come into Exile.

Before Judge Kenneth King, 36th District Court,
in pro per

THE HONORABLE ELENA HERRADA, ELECTED SCHOOL BOARD IN EXILE:

I have never been arrested before for any reason.
It has become necessary to confront immoral legal authority.
If we do nothing, we are complicit.
As an elected school board member, I have been sued by the attorney general of Michigan for being elected.
Judges, lawyers, teachers, politicians, and citizens are afraid to speak out against this abuse of power.
The rich do not have to pay taxes and are able to evict residents from their apartments and homes without a hearing.
Sports arenas and casinos take precedence over schools.
Privately owned party buses roam the streets while Detroiters wait for public busses that never come.
Taxes are waved for the rich while the poorest are left holding the bag.
Lighting is privatized, and we are still in the dark.

Police, firefighters, and city workers who have carried us for generations are threatened with losing their hard-earned pensions, so bond holders who did nothing to earn them are stealing them.

Thieves are allowed to open charter schools and crooks are imposed upon the elected school board by the power-mad emergency manager.

The library is in danger of being looted by well-dressed criminals.

Honest citizens and elected school board members and library commissioners are demonized by the bought and paid for media.

We are told we will elect Duggan, who never suffered any of the degradations Detroiters have been suffering.

People of good will eventually go into exile with us.

The elected school board has suffered under this tyranny for the past five years and now we are told we have another eighteen months. There is no end to the looting until we run out these banks. They are never going to be satisfied.

Detroit must stand up.

REV. BILL WYLIE-KELLERMANN, PASTOR, ST. PETER'S EPISCOPAL DETROIT

As a native Detroiter, a graduate of Detroit Public Schools, a pastor and thirty-five-year resident in southwest Detroit, this city is home to my heart. As a community activist committed to nonviolence I have been arrested many times in a forty-year history of direct action in antiwar, solidarity, labor, environmental, and antinuclear struggles. And so I have been wishing for resistance actions against the unconstitutional and illegitimate authority of these emergency managements. I'm praying for it now.

We were present in City Council chambers on April 16 to break the pall of silence when the contract with the Jones Day law firm was up for council approval. We knelt and sang and would not cease . . .

Because gathering signatures and passing a repeal ballot measure are made to be meaningless exercises;

Because the disasters of financial emergency are contrived and concocted;

Because, like our public schools, our city is being dismantled by design;

Because the dominating spell of a legal fiction has been cast over this city;

Because the City Council willingly exercises only the power allowed it by the forces of emergency management;

Because the multimillion-dollar Jones Day contract was an open conflict of interest and an act of public malfeasance;

Because the emergency manager claims authority to make that contract himself and did not need the council to do so, the majority gave comfort, cover, and the appearance of democratic rule;

Because this law firm, third largest in the world, serves and represents the very banks and financial institutions that hold Detroit hostage, and because Kevin Orr, a partner in this firm, negotiated the arrangement;

Because their client, Bank of America/Merrill Lynch, far bigger than the city of Detroit, holds it hostage with indebtedness and credit swaps; and because the restructurers offer Detroit pensioners ten cents on the dollar while offering Bank of America seventy-five cents on the dollar;

Because it was, it is, time for the people of Detroit to withdraw their consent and cooperation;

Because if nothing else we need to go on record; because there must be a history of conscience to tell our young people and children.

2014

Detroit: Is Your City Next?

THE CATHOLIC WORKER, NEW YORK CITY,
JANUARY–FEBRUARY 2014

Christ drove the money lenders out of the temple. But today nobody dares to drive the money lenders out of the temple . . . because the money lenders have taken a mortgage on the temple. —Peter Maurin

Let me tell you about a new form of urban fascism, one which is the template for direct corporate rule. Though it comports fully with what is happening in most of the global south, this despotism called emergency management is being deployed in Michigan, and Detroit is its major test ground. Since March of 2013 we have been living under a non-elected government thoroughly allied with the banks and corporations.

Start with the political structure: an emergency manager (EM) appointed by the governor over a municipality or school district holds in their person all the powers of government plus more. In a city, the EM immediately supplants the mayor and City Council, eliminating even those checks and balances. So an emergency manager can write laws with the stroke of a pen, repeal ordinances, fire employees, set budgets, sell assets, privatize services and departments—and, two further extraordinary powers, unilaterally break contracts, whether union or otherwise, and even rewrite the city charter. Though Detroit is much in the news, you are not likely get this from broadcast media, from reading the Detroit dailies, or the *Times* for that matter.

In the fall of 2013 organizers got 250,000 signatures to put the repeal of the EM law on the ballot, but it had to go to the State Supreme Court to overrule the board of canvasser's decision that the typeface of the title was microns too small. It was repealed by 2.3 million citizens, including 81 percent of Detroit, but the lame duck Republican legislature turned around and re-passed a ballot-proof version. I'm not making this up.

This legislation comes full blown out of the right-wing think tanks. As the cover of *Time* magazine put it over an image of the Detroit skyline: "Is Your City Next?" They were referring to municipal bankruptcy, but it applies equally to emergency management. Most of my adult life I've lived under Phil Berrigan's adage, "If voting could change anything, they'd make it illegal." Now here I am resisting the big assault on local democracy.

RACE AND DEVASTATION

How is this happening? Because so far it's being done almost entirely in African American cities. In fact, at this point every major black city in the state but one are under emergency managers. Over half the African American population of the state of Michigan is under non-elected governments. And three-quarters of the black elected officials in Michigan have been replaced by this process. Even if many of the managers are black, as in Detroit, the exercise is fundamentally racist. Constitutional and Voting Rights Act lawsuits have been filed in federal court, but as of this writing they are stayed from going forward.

When one of the Detroit dailies publishes an editorial entitled "Can Detroit Govern Itself?," decoding the subtext is simple: "Can black people rule themselves?" White folks out-of-state shake their heads and shrug indifference. Problem is, once the mechanisms are perfected and the precedents are set, emergency management will be coming to a white city near you.

Even many black folks in Detroit, steeped in news mainly from our broadcast media, buy into the view. This black majority city just elected its first white mayor in nearly fifty years. He lived all that time in Livonia, known as "the whitest city in America," moved into Detroit last year too late to be properly on the primary ballot, but won by a landslide as a write-in candidate. Running as an outsider with connections to turn things around, he won the final election with so much corporate money he didn't know where to put it all.

Detroit's financial crisis has structural causes to be sure, and there's no surprise that race is a factor here as well. With de-industrialization, job flight and capital flight have long eroded the tax base. In the last decade over a quarter million auto-related jobs have disappeared from the metro area. But beginning in the fifties, white flight decimated the city's population. A million people left. Even before the foreclosure crisis nearly one third of the housing stock had been lost to flight. Detroit has gone from being the city with the highest rate of homeownership in the nation, to the city with the highest foreclosure rate. As elsewhere, predatory mortgages were heavily targeted toward black neighborhoods, which contributes to losing another quarter of the population in just the last decade.

Also, by state decree, folks in the suburbs working in Detroit do not have their city taxes taken out by employers. They stiff the city to the tune of $140 million a year. Cash flow is affected. The corporations in Detroit also stiff the city on taxes and fees. City Councilwoman JoAnn Watson estimates the amount in arrears to be some $800 million. One noteworthy tax scoff is the owner of the Tigers and the Red Wings, who owes tens of million by himself. But he's getting a bond measure to build a new hockey rink and is being given the land to boot. Emergency management makes that work.

Oh ,the contradictions of my life. Here I am a lifelong, conscientious war tax resister bemoaning tax refusers (though neither conscientious nor honorable). I've always paid local taxes, but now even I think, "Taxation without representation?"

DISASTER CAPITALISM

We are at a moment when capitalism, reaching certain limits, may be seen turning inward to devour basic institutions like public education and now municipalities. What's been done globally is coming home.

If Detroit were an indebted third world nation, what is being imposed on us (privatization of assets and services, deregulation, and austerity budgets) would be called "structural adjustment." The economists out of the University of Chicago, who hatched this formula decades ago, discovered that the quickest way to impose it was in the wake of a natural disaster (tsunami, earthquake, hurricane). Devastation is opportunity. Then it dawned on them that disasters could also be created. Think of Detroit as New Orleans with a different kind of storm.

In Detroit public education under emergency management is being dismantled and replaced with for-profit cyber school charters. Private security roams downtown looking like cops; their surveillance cameras feed a wall of monitors not at police headquarters, but in a corporate office. The mayor wants a big downtown firm to serve as the "law department." The bus system and lighting are in private hands, as is the Health Department. A few weeks ago the Worker soup kitchen at St. Peter's got our first visit from Not the Health Department. We knew the old inspector by name and face. The new contractor thinks we are a restaurant. New sinks have gone in—one just inside the kitchen door so guests can wash their hands before crossing the threshold to use the phone.

Detroit does have a cash flow crisis, roughly $200 million per year. But that has also been partly manufactured. Governor Snyder, with help from his Republican legislature, has worsened the crisis under review by cutting $67 million in state revenue sharing with the city. Last year Detroiters passed a bond measure of $137 million to address cash flow but while he was weighing whether Detroit was in crisis, the governor held the monies in escrow. The city unions negotiated with the mayor a package which would have saved Detroit over $100 million, but the governor effectively prevented it from coming to the council for approval.

Which leads to the moneylenders, as Peter Maurin would say. He would be amazed (well, perhaps not) at the extent to which debt is aggressively marketed to students, homeowners, consumers, institutions, and yes, municipalities.

In Detroit, the same banks (Bank of America to name one) that have been "devouring widows' houses," eating out housing stock with predatory loans from below, have managed predatory loans from above as well. I won't try to explain "interest rate swaps" here, but suffice it to say that at a time when banks get their money at near zero interest, Detroit is paying the banks at a rate of 6 percent or more. As insiders to the bubble and crash they knew the day was coming and were even able to manipulate the international base rate, so the decks were stacked.

Couldn't we get out of this deal? Or some of it? The city could seek charges of criminal fraud (like Oakland did). Or an honest bankruptcy could reduce or renegotiate it. But instead the emergency manager has put forward a criminal alternative: borrow $350 million from Barclay's of London; use $250 million of that to buy Bank of America out of the deal (they've already gotten $800 million); the other hundred million is roughly the cost of legal fees for the bankruptcy. What would Barclay's get from the deal? If it goes through, Detroit is on the hook for the $350 million and interest (20 percent of the city budget for the next six years) and they get first dibs on major city assets to be sold, like the Water Department that serves the three-county urban sprawl, or tracts of land, perhaps even the city's jewel of an island park so long coveted by developers. And then, as Glenn Ford notes: "To ensure that the city can never escape the clutches of capital, the contract would allow Barclay's to immediately declare Detroit in default if Emergency Financial Manager rule is ended for any reason—that is, the corporate plan calls for the permanent cessation of democracy in Detroit."

DETROIT HAS NOT DECLARED BANKRUPTCY

Make no mistake. Though they are referred to in court and the media as "the city," it is the governor and the EM who have filed for bankruptcy. When a city files, the judge puts a stay on any suits against the city. However, in this case he has put a stay on the constitutional and Voting Rights Act challenges to the state's emergency management law in federal court. The logic is this: first we'll do the bankruptcy, then they can figure out if the EM had the legal standing to even file it.

If the city filed for bankruptcy, and was arguing in its own interest, the banks and the pensioners and the unions would all be on a level playing field. Instead the banks have been dealt with up front, offered eighty cents on the dollar. The city pensioners were offered ten cents. Pensions are actually protected by the state constitution, but the judge has rule that is trumped by US corporate law.

Though he's running the entire city, Emergency Manager Kevyn Orr is a bankruptcy lawyer. He oversaw Chrysler's Chapter 11. Back channel emails uncovered last summer show him being courted before the financial emergency was even ruled. He expressed concern that it appears the EM law was written expressly for bankruptcy. But he took the job. He resigned as a partner of Jones Day, third largest law firm in the world, among whose primary clients are, you guessed it, Bank of America/Merrill Lynch—bigger clients for them than the City of Detroit. Just days before Orr's appointment was announced, Jones Day was named by the city as the law firm to restructure the city's debt. Actually to restructure the city. They are now the lawyers in the governor's bankruptcy case. They bill us at $1,000 per hour. The firm will make about $100 million.

THE LAST VESTIGE OF DEMOCRACY AND CREATING OUR OWN

A local campaign (with a development plan) is named Opportunity Detroit. It sees the city as a housing space, a high-tech corridor, and a destination for sports and entertainment and that is how the city is being restructured not just financially but spatially. Certain areas, like along the riverfront or major transport spines, are being resourced for corporate development, while outlying neighborhoods are having the plug pulled on lights and infrastructure. When the archdiocese was preparing last year for another wave of top-down church closings, the cardinal first met with the mayor to find out which neighborhoods had no future. The foundations and their ancillary non-profit agencies are in on the mapping (they were recently called into a closed-door meeting with the bankruptcy judge on a similar premise). People lose their homes and neighborhoods not to eminent domain, but simply because the resources—schools, churches, police, fire, lights, and water—are being pulled out from under them. Land empties and spaces open up. The forested gated communities of the future are being designed.

The neighborhood of my church, St. Peter's, is one being resourced. Hip destination restaurants pop up. Downtown corporations pay employees to move in here. The new street lights will have surveillance cameras built in and networked. Meanwhile, the Worker soup kitchen is a liability to be closed or harassed out. Our guests are stopped to be frisked, ticketed, and criminalized, driven out of town in police cars, suffer violence. They are to make way for opportunity.

Though I am more accustomed to arrests at SAC bases, White House gates, or missile factories, my last was in City Council chambers. It was the morning they ratified the Jones Day contract and also the fiftieth anniversary of Martin Luther King's "Letter from a Birmingham Jail." We held up the vote. We blocked aisles and sang "We Shall Not be Moved." As spectators and speakers joined us the crowd swelled and the harmonies turned rich and deep. But only two of us were arrested. I was. And the other arrested, an elected member of the school board, cried "Shame!" while being hauled away. The police, whose jobs and pensions are on the line, thanked us at the precinct. Come trial, their testimony will be of interest. We have asked for a jury trial and it's scheduled for January 27. A jury is the last vestige of democracy in Detroit. We will remind them so. That is, the last vestige other than those we create ourselves, participatory and from below. Everything we do these days must build community and democratic practice.

We know that it is a moment to resist displacement, emergency management, gentrification, corporate occupation. It is also a moment, exiled in our own city, to build and plant and marry. To make real community and practice real democracy. But that's another story to write and to tell.

2014

January 4, 2014
FOR IMMEDIATE RELEASE:
Jones Day is Not Detroit

Detroit activist pastor Rev. William Wylie-Kellermann was removed from the Detroit bankruptcy court trial yesterday by security for speaking truth to power.

The incident occurred at about 11:30 AM on Friday, January 3, 2014, the first day of resumed trial proceedings before Judge Steven Rhodes, on the December 24 settlement proposal to pay Bank of America/Merrill Lynch and UBS bank $165 million, borrowed from Barclays bank, to settle claims over dubious interest rate "swaps." Emergency Manager Kevyn Orr was on the stand.

Judge Rhodes denied a creditor motion by attorney Caroline English of Ambac Assurance Corporation to compel production of attorney/client privileged documents relied on by Emergency Manager Kevyn Orr, regarding the evaluation of Detroit's legal claims against these "counterparties."

At that point, Rev. Wylie-Kellermann addressed the court directly from his seat at the back of the room: *"Judge Rhodes, even without these documents it's clear that Bank of America should be sued and prosecuted, not compensated."* He added as he was physically removed from the room by court security, *"Jones Day is not the City of Detroit!"* Judge Rhodes immediately ran from the bench out of the court, and the proceedings were briefly halted.

Rev. Wylie-Kellermann, of St. Peter's Episcopal Church, Michigan and Trumbull in Detroit, left the building with a few others shortly after the incident. He explained his nonviolent direct action: *"For the people of Detroit by throwing its authority behind Kevyn Orr, this court has the same legitimacy as the Emergency Manager and Jones Day: none. The filing is illegitimate, unconstitutional, immoral, and against the will of the people. The court has become an instrument of direct corporate rule. The Barclays loan is the 'swap' of one theft for another. In a legitimate court, Bank of America would be prosecuted for such a predatory scheme, not compensated."*

Rev. Wylie-Kellermann and Detroit School Board in exile member Elena Herrada still face misdemeanor charges in Thirty-Sixth District Court on January 27, 2014, for disrupting the Detroit City Council vote on the Jones Day contract with Detroit in April 2013. They have repeatedly demanded a jury trial on those charges, but Detroit—governed by former Jones Day partner and Emergency Manager Kevyn Orr—has repeatedly refused to proceed with the prosecution. Jones Day also represents the counterparties—Bank of America/Merrill Lynch and UBS—to be paid in the deal at issue.

2014

Station: New Introductory—
Where you put your body

At the Passover meal in Jerusalem, Jesus says, "This is my body given for you." How he gives and where he puts his body is the key to the Jerusalem events, and for us in the passion.

At the beginning of the week, with masses of people afoot, he turns the Passover liberation pilgrimage into a march on the temple, straight to the currency exchange, that intersection of the imperial and local economies. This he names a den of gangsters. And there with his own hands he turns over the tables, bodily exorcising (casting out) the money changers. Then it is said, he occupies the temple, allowing no one to carry any goods through its courts.

Day after day he returns to the scene of the direct action crime, sitting down to teach—about the authority to do such things, about imperial tax resistance, about the freedom of the resurrection. He puts his body in places surveilled and patrolled. The authorities mark his body for death.

Infiltrated and betrayed, with the cops and authorities on the way, he agonizes in the garden over whether to be driven from town, to flee quietly or to stay. He stays to drinks the cup.

Now his body is bound, controlled, judged, humiliated, condemned, tortured, ritually executed. The assaults to it are told in close detail.

In death his body remains an object of contention. Is it yet a corpse? Will it violate the Sabbath? Who can request burial rights? Can the women properly anoint it? Will it be stolen by the discipleship movement? Or can the stone be set with an official seal and the body guarded with troops?

The resurrection is also about the body. Will his body stay dead? Stay put? Hush up? Or will it walk free? Speak truth?

Today we ask, where is the body of Christ? Where is it suffering? But that begs the question: where will we put our bodies? In what spaces, for what love, and with what freedom?

2014

Station: Banks and Bankruptcy

"Beware . . . . They devour widows' houses and for the sake of appearance say long prayers. They will receive the greater condemnation." He looked up and saw rich people putting their tithes into the treasury; he also saw a poor widow put in two small copper coins. He said, *"Truly I tell you, this poor widow has put in more than all of them; for all of them have contributed out of their abundance, but she out of her poverty has put in all she had to live on."* When some were speaking about the temple, how it was adorned with beautiful stones and gifts dedicated to God, he said, *"As for these things that you see, the days will come when not one stone will be left upon another; all will be thrown down."* (Luke 20:45–21:6)

In the time of Jesus the temple was effectively the bank. It was controlled by the Sadducees, pro-Roman landed aristocrats, the 1 percent absentee owners. Widows' houses and peasant lands were being devoured by high taxes and runaway interest. Records of indebtedness (the mortgage paper) was held in the temple treasury. When the Zealots took over in 67 AD they burned the treasury and released the debts. The money-changing tables marked the place where the Roman money economy met the local. When Jesus goes up to Jerusalem, he marches straight to the money market and sends the coins spilling out the door. It is then they decide to kill him.

In Detroit, the banks—like Bank of America—have devoured the substance of our neighborhoods with racially targeted predatory loans, driving people from their homes. Already bailed out, they make money foreclosing homes and thereby receiving the insured purchase value. The same banks —like Bank of America—hold the Detroit's people and resources hostage to municipal predatory loans, the so-called interest swaps. They are regularly represented by Jones Day, the third largest law firm in the world. It's the firm that is supposed to represent the city in bankruptcy court. They propose cuts in pension payments, all that some widows have to live on, in order to pay the banks. To negotiate with their own clients is a criminal conflict of interest. The law firm stands to make some $100 million on the bankruptcy.

Verse: *Were you there when they stole my life and home?*

2014

Poem: A Wager of Love

Charity Hicks was a water, food, and environmental justice organizer in Detroit. In May she sparked the current struggle against the massive water shutoffs, by resisting her own. When the contractor had no order she called the police and they arrested her. In the days after she urged Detroiters to "wage love" in the resistance movement, and helped initiate the filing of the United Nations complaint that resulted in the declaration that the shutoffs were a violation of the human right to potable water. In New York to speak on a panel, she was struck by a hit-and-run driver while waiting for a bus. After weeks in a coma she crossed over to God. In the wake of her death, pastors, religious leaders, and allies circulated a public letter against the shutoffs. A number of them were arrested in a series of actions blocking the trucks from going out to do so. Bill Wylie-Kellermann was among them.

The Greatest of These: Wage Love
Of Charity, July 2014

like water
poured out, soaking the earth
Charity Hicks was a libation upon us.

tradition says: the blood of the martyrs is the seed
    of the church, the struggle, the movement, the community beloved
    do not hesitate to call her a martyr

    to call her blood such a witness, her life such a seed
    her voice such a mighty water
    or her righteousness one with the ever flowing stream

I loved the curl of her lip when truth was on it.
like Sophia/Wisdom she took her place at the gate and cried out.
once in an audience at a downtown event on gentrification
    where questions and comments were to be tweeted by the techno-gentry
    then fell as designer digital fountains behind the panel—
    she wasn't having it—spoke aloud, uppity and out of turn
    summoning our silenced voices to speech.

there was the unspeakable gut-rocking silence (induced, uninduced) of
the Bellevue ICU;
    partner and friends drawn close, still reading and singing
    prayers to defy the accidental designs of demonic providence.
    in the deep sleep at the end of days, she hears it all, every last word.
    the prayers to come home and walk among us. and she does.

Gone to God and the ancestors, this old soul, this elder born
    comes walking bold, color and fabric thrown high.
    she carries herself with dignity and authority
    won perhaps from ancient royalty, but more
    by the rooted planting of barefoot step in a D-town garden
    history and memory alive beneath her feet
    when fruits come in and street harvest is shared
she summons: stand there and tell history
stand there and write policy
stand there and convene the people

where are the preachers? she once asked, gently calling me out.
it was just days after her release from central detention
cuffed and hauled off for resisting her own water shutoff.
the moment she sparked Detroit's water revolt and its community
movement.
at her committal I assisted: earth to earth,
and heard again the question poured upon me.

she knew there are wagers of death collecting chips they never played
    reaching business-like, with a murderous hand.
she could look them in the eye without flinching or failing
throw down the chain, name the theft.
she made a wager of love, betting her life without restraint or regret.
there on the street on the way to speak, vulnerable and indestructible, she rose up
this wager of truth
this wager of memory
this beloved wager of love.

2014

Her Name Was Charity: The Detroit Water Struggle

The Catholic Worker, New York City, October–November 2014

Think of Charity Hicks as the Rosa Parks of the Detroit Water Struggle. She was arrested in Detroit early on May 16 for resisting the shutoff of her own water. The private contractor came early in the morning, but she was up. Since he was hitting a bunch of people on her block she went door to door rousing people to say: he's coming; fill your tub, fill pots and pans! Then, because she still had two more days to settle her bill she demanded to see the shut off order. He had none, only a list of addresses. When the altercation turned physical she called the police. Let it be said that Charity was a forceful, even loud when required, black woman. She had a large persona. The white cops who arrived averred that she "needed to be taught a lesson" and instead arrested her. They left her house open and threw her phone and keys on the front lawn. She was essentially disappeared.

Because of the situation in Detroit, arrestees are no longer taken to the precinct. They go directly to a Central Detention Center run by the State of Michigan in a former prison within city boundaries. Still barefoot and bleeding she was put into a holding area with thirty other women. One toilet. No benches. Find a place on the floor not covered with blood or vomit. It's the weekend so you'll be arraigned by video to a court in Romulus.

When her husband returned home and saw the remains of the situation he began calling local hospitals to try to find her. Eventually he went to the police station to file a missing persons report. They said: we have her.

Visits and bond attempts were turned away. Because she is a diabetic and was going into sugar shock, frantic lawyers were able to get her out on a *habeas corpus* motion. But, truth be told, they had arrested the wrong person. Charity Hicks was a food, water, and environmental justice activist in Detroit. Strong and articulate. A woman not to be messed with.

Two days later she told this story at St. Peter's Episcopal Church. She urged the gathered activists, in a now famous phrase, to "wage love" in the water struggle for justice. The occasion was the presence of Nelson and Joyce Johnson, two faith-rooted activists from North Carolina. Nelson had been wounded by Klan members in the 1979 Geensboro Massacre. Since then they have, among other things, founded the Beloved Community Center and shepherded the first truth and reconciliation process on US soil. They were also instrumental in the recent Moral Mondays campaign where week after week groups have been arrested at the State House in Raleigh for resisting the right-wing assault on all social programs and budgets. They were here to discuss the connections between the North Carolina efforts and the struggle in Detroit against emergency management.

An emergency manager appointed by Governor Snyder has all the powers of government and more in his person: He can write ordinances, repeal laws, fire employees, set budgets, privatize departments, sell city assets, break union contracts, rewrite the city charter, and file for bankruptcy. Or so we are told. The law justifying this was repealed in a ballot measure be Michigan citizens, but the lame duck Republican legislature re-passed a worse version within months. At this point every black city in the state is under the emergency manager law. Over half the black citizens of Michigan are under non-elected governments. Seventy-five percent of the black elected officials have been replaced by emergency managers. The Detroit Public Schools have been under one for five years and they have been successfully dismantled, privatized, and destroyed a la New Orleans.

Under the emergency manager the Detroit Water and Sewage Department had announced in March that it was beginning to shut off water to anyone more than two months or $150 dollars behind on their bill. A hundered and twenty thousand homes. They were shooting for something like 3,000 per week. A couple years back, $500 million in bond money for infrastructure repairs had been turned over to the banks to buy out the predatory and illegal credit swaps into which the department had entered. Now in the effort to privatize Detroit water, poor people were going to have to pay up or be expelled. At the same time, this comported with the reorganizing of Detroit neighborhoods, resourcing some and pulling the plug on others. People not expelled by mortgage and tax foreclosures, or by the disappearance of schools, precincts, and fire stations, could now be sent packing by water shutoffs.

Neslon and Joyce thought something like this might be planned for North Carolina as well. When Nelson heard Charity's story, he said: this is it. In the picture of a child or elder holding a cup at an empty faucet, all the connections can be made. He said this is the thing that can both deepen and broaden the Detroit movement. He drew a map of campaign on a paper plate. He was prophetic in every sense of the word. What he mapped and foresaw has come to be.

Within the week Charity was at a conference planned by the Peoples' Water Board in Detroit with Maude Barlowe, a Canadian writer and water activist who had been instrumental in getting the United Nations to declare access to potable water a human right. When she heard Charity's story, she said: this is it. We need to file a complaint with the United Nations. Within weeks UN representatives had announced that to cut off water to people because they were unable to pay was indeed a violation of basic human rights. That got a lot of international attention and soon local Detroit papers and TV stations were forced to cover the story themselves.

Charity had been invited to North Carolina to tell the story, but first she went to New York City to speak about the crisis at the Left Forum. While waiting at a bus stop, on her way to speak, she was hit by a car that jumped the curb and struck her down. A hit and run. She was in a coma for weeks. In early July she crossed over to God and the ancestors.

A group of religious leaders and allies began circulating a letter against the shutoffs and privatization and in support of the Peoples Affordability Plan of 2005 that would set water prices according to ability to pay. Drawing from interfaith tradition, they said water is a grace, a gift of the Creator, beneath everything. It is the lifeblood of the planet circulating in river and rain. As a gift of God is belongs to all creatures equally. In tradition it is part of the commons for which we are stewards. This view is represented legally in the idea that water is not a utility or a commodity, but a public trust, held for all the people. It is represented in the idea that you can't own a body of water, even if you own the land around it. Any high school kid knows if you are walking on the beach and someone tells you to get off their property, you step into the water and you're off. It is also represented in the idea that water is a human right—it belongs accessibly to everyone. The faith letter was signed by five bishops and eighty religious leaders in the city, plus many more in the region and nationally. It was hand delivered to the Water Board, the Detroit City Council, and to the shutoff contractor.

Meanwhile people started protesting every Friday at the Detroit Water Board. They called it Freedom Fridays, echoing the Moral Mondays movement in North Carolina.

In the days that followed Charity's death a group of ten people decided to take direct action and block the trucks from going out to shut the water off. They went to the gates of Homrich Wrecking, the private contractor with a $5.6 million contract to turn off the water. The company is paid by the shutoff, so they are incentivized to do as many as they can, as fast as they can. We dedicated our action to the memory and spirit of Charity Hicks. For two hours we blocked the gates. In a very physical confrontation, we were arrested and taken to the Central Detention Facility. So far, this was pretty much how Nelson Johnson had diagramed it on his paper plate.

The following week ten more people went back. This time we blocked the drive and stopped the trucks for seven hours before being arrested. The same day downtown, more than a thousand people marched from Cobo Hall to Bank of America to City Hall to Hart Plaza to protest the shutoffs. A union, National Nurses United, came forward to support the march and declare the situation in Detroit a public health crisis. When water is shut off people can't cook, wash, or flush toilets. On top of that sometimes they lose their children to Protective Services because the situation is made unhealthy and unsafe.

In response We the People of Detroit set up a hotline for folks who have been shut off to call (844-42WATER) and began to organize stations around the city to provide emergency water and information. Our church, where the Worker kitchen resides, is one of them. On July 24 the council of Canadians, led by Maude Barlowe, delivered 300 gallons of water to our water station in an act of solidarity. We stacked the water around our baptismal font at the back of the church and declared it a place of grace. A week later Keepers of the Mountain in West Virginia (where a chemical spill had left an entire town without water) delivered 1,100 gallons of water. Another, even larger shipment, is expected from a UAW local in Chicago. The support is growing.

Hence, the Detroit emergency manager has a problem. The federal judge in Detroit's bankruptcy called in the Water Board to say, this has become an issue for the bankruptcy trial. (It already was deeply embedded.) You're making the city look bad. So the Water Board declared a two-week moratorium on shutoffs. Whereafter the emergency manager announced that he was giving administration of the Water Department over to Detroit's mayor, Mike Duggan. Duggan is white and was "elected" in a landslide of write-in votes. He can't do anything the emergency manager doesn't permit, but they work pretty closely together. Think of it as good cop–bad cop. The mayor says things that have been handled badly under the emergency manager, but now we'll do them right. He has a ten-point plan to extend the shutoff moratorium, to give people time to pay up, to hold some informational events, and to crack down on those "stealing" water. There isn't anything in it about the $29 million owed by commercial and industrial accounts, and not a word about the Water Affordability Plan.

No one took Nelson's paper plate and followed the design. It's all just happened in a very decentralized and Spirit-led way. Charity Hicks walks among us and we are "waging love." As this is written, the bankruptcy trial is scheduled to begin after Labor Day. More actions are being discerned. The story is not over yet.

2014

Water Letter: Religious Leaders and Allies

Ho, everyone who thirsts, come to the waters
Let the one who has no money, come . . . . (Isaiah 55:1)

Friends in Faith and Fellow Citizens:

In our traditions water is a free grace, part of the great gift that underlies all creation. We drink it as life itself. We wade through it to freedom. And in conversion we are immersed and sprinkled and cleansed. In season we know to honor it even by fasting from it. It is the lifeblood of the planet, circulating as rain and river. Water is the very emblem of the commons, what we hold together as one. We share it beholden to local indigenous peoples who understood, understand this deeply. For governments that serve the people, a water system is a public trust, held in trust for this generation and those to come. For the United Nations access to clean potable water is counted a human right.

In Detroit the largest basin of fresh water in the world flows by us through the river, the strait.

But in Detroit, under emergency management, as many as 150,000 homes are threatened with shutoff, up to 3,000 per week, largely by private contractors. People, including children, the elderly, and infirm, wake up in the morning to find themselves unable to drink, cook, wash, or flush toilets. In fact, two-thirds of these homes are occupied by children. People without water fear losing their children to Protective Services. They can be driven from their homes, their neighborhood, their city.

On June 18, 2014 a complaint charging a violation of human rights was filed with the United Nations. Three special rapporteurs have already responded in a written statement, stressing the urgency of the situation: "Disconnection of water services because of failure to pay due to lack of means constitutes a violation of the human right to water and other international human rights."

As religious leaders and communities we join our voices to say: in the name of humanity stop the shutoffs.

To Detroiters we say, alert, defend, and protect your neighbors from shutoff. To faith communities we say, become stations of water distribution (for information and guidance on this call 1-844-42WATER), as well as places of education, community, and resistance. To water workers, we say refuse to cut off your fellow citizens. To the Water Board, we say reverse this inhuman policy: turn their water back on. To the City Council, we say stop compounding this travesty with rate increases and other complicity. Revive and implement the Water Affordability Program. To the governor we say: cease privatization and call off this action taken under emergency management.

To our God we pray, defend the children, the least, the poor. Help us to do so this day. Let your justice roll down like waters and righteousness like an ever-flowing stream.

2014

Sixty Years Later. In Detroit the End of Brown: Separate and Unequal

ON THE EDGE (DETROIT CATHOLIC WORKER), WINTER 2014

The Detroit Public Schools are being dismantled by design and effectively looted. Though Detroiters and the elected school board are consistently blamed for their demise, for twelve of the last fifteen years DPS has been under state control.

Mother Helen Moore, an attorney who heads the Education Task Force, has become notorious for her fight on behalf of the schools, and tells the story over and over in community meetings. It's well documented.

When the Detroit schools were first taken over in 1999, enrollment was stable (at 200,000 students), test scores were middle range compared to state averages and rising, an "Afro-centric" curriculum developed by the district over a number of years was in use, there was a $93 million budget surplus, and $1.2 billion from a bond issue intended by residents for building improvements. It was the latter, not any financial emergency, which drew the takeover. Then-Governor Engler was determined that those improvement dollars not go to local minority contractors, but to suburban and out-of-state builders. Follow the money.

When control was returned to the board seven years later, the fund deficit was $200 million, enrollment had dropped to 118,000, the curriculum was gone, as was the bond money spent at shamefully inflated prices. One hundred million simply disappeared without audit or indictment. This is the background of emergency management in Detroit.

The elected board was returned to power in early 2006 with the burden of a deficit budget under which they labored for three years, including the 2008 economic collapse caused by the financial industry. The first emergency financial manager, Robert Bobb (not an educator but a developer famous for brokering deals, and supported by Eli Broad if you know what that means), was put in place on the premise of a $135 million budget deficit. When he left the deficit had ballooned to $327 million and test scores had plummeted to among the worst in the nation. He was paid an annual salary of half a million dollars. Get the drift?

DISASTER CAPITALISM AND PUBLIC EDUCATION

We are at a point in late capitalism where corporations are turning inward to devour other corporations (hostile takeovers), municipalities (as in the Detroit bankruptcy), and basic social institutions (like education—public education in particular).

Globally, the architects of structural adjustment (austerity budgets, deregulation, selling off public assets, and privatization) had discovered that natural disasters afforded the best opportunities for quick takeover. With respect to education, the Katrina flooding is the example of opportunity provided—where New Orleans public education was effectively replaced by a profitable charter system. But they also discovered that disasters could be manufactured as well. We've experienced this in Detroit both as a city and as a school system. Defund. Make it fail or appear to do so. Take it over.

THE OTHER EMERGENCY MANAGEMENT IN DETROIT

Because of the bankruptcy recently completed, emergency management as a form of urban fascism is better known at the municipal level in Detroit. However, the public schools have been under emergency management now for five years. The destruction and dismantling of that system is what now bodes for the city as a whole.

Though Public Act 436, which allegedly authorizes emergency management, allows that elected bodies taken over and supplanted may vote after eighteen months to put out an EM, the courts have ruled that this means the governor simply has to install a new and different EM. Emergency management is a permanent feature of black cities in Michigan.

The elected and unpaid school board, though constantly tarred in the media with corruption or incompetence or simply ignored, has continued to function "in exile" as a body conscientiously accountable to parents, students, and citizens, consistently resisting takeover. (Would that our city council had an ounce of such vision or fiber!) Believe it or not, the state attorney general sued the district representatives on the board for being elected. Since they were duly seated and sworn in, the maneuver failed. Now a foundation-funded and nonprofit-orchestrated campaign seeks to oust them altogether for a structure of "mayoral control."

Emergency management has been the blunt instrument of privatization. More than half the schools in Detroit are charters. Though originally conceived as vehicles for creativity, charters have become a mainstay for union-busting and privatization. In the industrial era schools prepared students for work in factory jobs, largely auto in Detroit. Now students are treated as state-funded commodities for extracting profits. The distinction between non-profit and for-profit charters is all but moot as even most of the former are managed by for-profit contractors. These schools compete with public schools, but have some choice in who they accept and who they don't; and they are not held to the same standards of accountability as public schools for teacher certification or even testing. In Detroit, headlines recently lamented that DPS had missed the deadline for federal funding of Headstart programs in the public schools. "Bungling black incompetence" is how that was read again in the suburbs—a loss of $4 million. But it was, of course, the governor's EM who missed the deadline. And not by accident: lo and behold, federal grants now fund Headstart as a privately contracted program in public school spaces.

Though parents were promised that more resources would be driven to the classroom, under emergency management administrative costs, actual and percentage wise, have nearly doubled: from $75 per pupil in 2008 to $143 per student today. Classroom size has taken a similar hit. Next year's budget has proposed the target of thirty-eight students per classroom be expanded to forty-three. With conflicts from such over-crowding, suspensions and expulsions go up; big contracts for restorative justice programs are justified. When a school board member pointed out that there weren't enough chairs in a classroom for that higher number, an administrator replied, "With the absenteeism rate that wouldn't be a problem."

Special schools, even fully funded ones, have simply closed: Oakman Orthopedic (a facility gorgeously built for disabled students—see

Kate Levy's film, *Because They Could: the Fight for Oakman School*) and The Day School for the Deaf (similarly equipped) are gone. Such buildings are abandoned or turned over wholesale to profiteers. Catherine Ferguson Academy, a school for pregnant teens and young mothers that had an international reputation for integrated urban agriculture, was handed over to a for-profit charter that simply gutted the program. (For a nostalgic look at the school see the film *Grown in Detroit*. It too will break your heart.) The building is now home to a Headstart program run by the sprawling nonprofit Southwest Solutions.

According to the *Detroit Free Press*, the second EM, Roy Roberts (also not an educator, but a retired auto exec), said he was told when he came that his job was to "blow up the Detroit Public Schools and dismantle it." So far so true.

RACIAL AND SPATIAL RESTRUCTURING

Detroit is being downsized and restructured geographically, as well as financially. The plug is being pulled on certain neighborhoods where poor black folks live. Predatory mortgages, now foreclosed, drive them out. Infrastructure is allowed to fail. Lights go out, fire stations close, cops withdraw. Water is shut off, pushing people out; and water bills are attached to tax indebtedness, forcing another round of foreclosures. And yes, schools close in neighborhoods slated to have no living future.

Resources, meanwhile, are going into other neighborhoods close to downtown, along the waterfront, or connected to the pending light rail. There are neighborhoods where young corporate-type white people are exuberantly moving in. It's their generation's turn! These are people generally without children, and don't yet care about schools. Who, without even a second thought, do not care about black children. Their indifference rules the day and the space.

THE EDUCATIONAL ACHIEVEMENT ("APARTHEID") AUTHORITY

"Authorities" are another mechanism for eviscerating, circumventing, and privatizing government. We have many of these para-governmental authorities in the city: the Downtown Development Authority controls funding and land, the Lighting Authority replaces the Lighting Department, the Great Lakes Water Authority essentially takes over the Detroit Water and Sewage Department and will likely hire Veolia, an international water corporation, to manage things. For two years we have not had a Health Department, but instead an Institute for Population Health. In like manner the EAA is not even properly an authority, but an inter-local agreement between Eastern Michigan University (where the governor appoints the university regents) and the Detroit Public Schools (where the governor appoints the emergency manager). Think of it as an agreement between the governor and the governor. And call it an authority, a "principality" if you will.

The EAA is supposed to be a state-wide school district for failing schools, but all of the schools are in Detroit. The idea was to take those in the lowest performing bottom 5 percent and turn them around. Two interesting coincidences: 1) almost all the students in failing school district are black and 2) when it came time to transfer the schools from Detroit to the EAA, the criterion seemed to be more a matter of which buildings had been newly renovated. One of the high schools transferred, Mumford, had been virtually rebuilt for $50.5 million. The building went to the EAA, but the reconstruction debt stayed with the DPS and comes out of the per student cost. Can you see how for DPS, those per pupil debt service costs went from $212 in 2008 to $1,109 per pupil today? Not having the debt service in the EAA means there is more money per pupil for the private contractors.

Forgive all the numbers, but just a few more. The chancellor of the EAA makes $325,000 per year (actually her total package approaches nearly half a million). She is new. The previous chancellor made the same amount, but he was forced to resign (but with a big severance package) under a scandal of corruption.

CYBER CURRICULA

In the era of the Gates Foundation and such, much of the sales and contractual profits to be made in education are technological: hard and soft. EAA students, almost entirely poor and black, have been test subjects for a new computer teaching program called Buzz. It came from Kansas City along with John Covington, first chancellor of the EAA. At a cost to the district of some $350,000, it is marketed as providing students with an individualized learning experience. (For this and what follows see Curt Guyette, "The EAA Exposed," *Detroit MetroTimes*.)

Textbooks left behind in the schools taken over by the EAA were simply thrown in the dumpster. Teachers in such EAA classroom are no longer teachers—they are facilitators only allowed to help students in using the program before them. One teacher, Brooke Harris at Mumford, was disciplined (she was eventually fired) for attempting to bring books and textbook-related materials into the classroom. "I was told that in the student-centered model, my role as teacher was primarily to supervise students to make sure they were using Buzz."

Speaking out as an EAA teacher is courageous and costly. In the EAA, no union provides protection from retaliation. They tend more often to speak circumspectly, as in these pages, or anonymously and off the record.

Individualized instruction can sound great, but exclusive use of the computer screen is an assault on community-based learning. There is no give and take in group discussion with a teacher.

On its website and in its ads, the EAA touts fantastic progress in bringing a greater percentage of students to proficiency levels in reading and math. And Covington was regularly on the road speaking at conferences to promote and market "the product."

Some of the evidence of shining performance was based on a test internally administered by the EAA. Teachers interviewed by the ACLU reported such pressure to produce positive test results that standard practice included allowing students to retake the test if they didn't do well the first time. Moreover, on the premise of individualized instruction and not wanting to "teach to the test," the EAA attempted to avoid its students even taking the state MEAP tests—even though it was MEAP scores which were used to justify its creation. Teaching to the test is, of course, a bad idea, but you can't have it both ways.

A close reading of MEAP test data released in February, however, shows that the majority of EAA students failed to demonstrate even marginal progress toward proficiency. Consider: 78 percent of students demonstrated no progress toward proficiency or even showed actual declines in math. The same was true for 58 percent of students in reading. Students who entered the system proficient had even grimmer results—the majority lost ground. (See Dr. Thomas Pedroni, *Detroit News*, April 21, 2014.) This, even though EAA students are held for longer days and year round.

The Buzz program, to be sure, was still being built and improved while it was tested on Detroit students. On a stipend basis, additional curriculum content was added by a team of eight teachers. Half of them were recent college graduates who had not studied to become teachers, had no certification or curriculum design experience, but had been given five weeks of training in the summer before coming to Detroit. They were part of the Teach for America program.

TEACH FOR AMERICA

When it opened for business, more than a quarter of the EAA's faculty were Teach for America students. TFA is a controversial non-profit designed to get new university graduates teaching in low-income urban and rural communities. Participants are encouraged in their college coursework to take education classes and pursue certification, though that is not required and most have not. For those not certified there is the intensive five weeks of training, plus structures of ongoing support, and simultaneous education courses. Military veterans are actively recruited. Participants make a two-year commitment. They come into any given school or district at the entry base salary, but combined with the AmeriCorps program, they receive federal loan forgiveness and vouchers toward further education. If there is a union they are not forbidden to join.

What's the problem? There is a narrative in circulation that bad teachers protected by unions and tenure are the problem. Though originally intended to fill teacher shortages in urban areas, the TFA program actually functions to replace veteran teachers. All teachers in EAA schools were terminated and required to reapply for their positions. More than a quarter of those were filled by TFA instructors fresh out of school. Do the math. There are no unions in EAA schools. The fact that studies are conducted comparing learning at the hands of veteran teachers vs. short-term recruits, suggests that replacement is part of the design. The for-profit charters are also full of TFA instructors, as are the public schools. With more of all to come.

Though TFA can be a shortcut into an ongoing teaching career, the two-year commitment, especially for those seeking loan forgiveness, graduate school funds, and resume experience, means recruits are not committed to a city, a school, or even a teaching vocation. The resignation rate in EAA schools has been extraordinarily high. Add TFA and you have a faculty in perpetual turnover.

African Americans comprise 13 percent of the TFA workforce. If those number hold in Detroit, it means students in a city that is 80 percent African American and in a failing school district that is virtually all black, are faced with teachers not from their culture, experience, or community. In a city where the young white savior narrative is already running strong, this is yet another version.

LATE BREAKING: MAYORAL CONTROL AND NEW ORLEANS COMPLETE?

As this issue goes to press there are moves in the lame duck Republican legislature to abolish the elected school board and put the public schools under direct mayoral control. The current mayor lived his entire life in a northern suburb, literally the whitest city in America. He was "elected" in a corporately funded write-in campaign, winning by a landslide. He was the treasurer of the EAA when an unaccounted "loan" of $12 million was given to it from DPS, but claims to be in the dark—to know nothing about it. A decade ago in a ballot measure Detroiters refused to give up the elected board to mayoral control. And more recently the City Council refused to put it again on the ballot. But like emergency management, it may simply be imposed. The difference between such a regime and emergency management is not worth talking about—simply more of the same. It's expected that this will pave the way for the entire system to be chartered and union representation ended altogether, bringing the New Orleans-style disaster to completion.

A DARK TIME

Though many are celebrating the bankruptcy, its structural adjustment, the giveaways of land and buildings and assets, the development dollars flowing, and the lucrative contracts to be had, this is a dark time for Detroit's children, poor, and black. They are being pushed down, pushed out, and pipelined toward prison. Sometimes I near despair. Still. There is hope in students who refuse to be so pushed and fight for their own education. There is hope in teachers who love Detroit's young and give themselves for them. There is hope in those who hold the line and struggle on their behalf, in going on record with a history of resistance. There's even hope in naming the darkness . . . and trusting the universe to bend toward light.

2015

Gentrification and Race: Can We Have a Real Conversation?

ON THE EDGE (DETROIT CATHOLIC WORKER), SPRING 2015

This morning guys came into the soup kitchen full of news that Kelly's Mission up the street (where a number of our guests find nightly shelter) had received an offer on the building. I wasn't surprised. A few weeks back I got a similar call from a well-heeled real estate agent in Farmington Hills asking, should the conditions be right, would I consider an offer and sell St. Peter's Church! He'd come by some time prior, and to him it looked like nothing much was going on here. He said, rude and presumptuous I thought, "I'm in the business of kissing frogs, and every once in a while one of them turns out to be a prince."

St. Peter's parish is in Corktown, first neighborhood westerly adjacent to downtown. It has been the "Catholic Worker neighborhood" if that phrase means anything to you—home to both the current Worker Community and an earlier incarnation, St. Francis House, begun by the Murphys perhaps sixty years ago. For the last thirty-five years St. Peter's has hosted Manna Community Meal, the Worker soup kitchen, and now houses St. Peter's water station, providing emergency water and information to any of the 33,000 Detroit homes whose water has been shut off in the last year.

We sit on Michigan Ave.—one of Detroit's "spoke streets," that, as Route 12 and the Red Arrow Highway, goes all the way to Chicago. Yes, Michigan Avenue along the water front in the Windy City is one and the same. It was once the Native Americans' Sauk Trail, though to be honest the Potowatomi and Anishinaabe peoples were themselves walking a game trail, one cut through the dense forest by mastodons and other creatures. Europeans turned it into a road, partly to accommodate military movements when the two waterfronts became fortified to claim and protect commerce and to enforce Indian removal as statehood loomed.

St. Peter's is kitty-corner from old Tiger Stadium, now a vast hole in the world, soon to be filled with a mixed-use development of Police Athletic League sports, upscale housing, and shops. Supported by a federal earmark of $3 million and recently approved as a project by the Detroit Economic Growth Corporation, its public announcement probably triggered the relator's speculative kisses.

Before our very eyes, our street, Michigan Avenue, is being redeveloped and gentrified. Looking west toward Kelley's there is among other things a new restaurant called Gold Cash Gold. Empty some years, it was once a pawn shop. The sign and the painted brick message are touched up and left as ironic nostalgia, acclaimed as a name, a quaint reminiscence of the days when poor people here bet their jewelry and their hopes on paying the rent and yet escaping debt to reclaim heirlooms and family memory. Now the menu suggests an appetizer: "Crispy pig ears, papaya chutney, house hot sauce, sorrel." It's proclaimed uniquely and locally Detroit. Whole hog. "Farmstead fine food with a nod to the South, rooted in old world tradition."

CORKTOWN AND CONQUISTADORS

Some six years ago, following a meeting with a group of new community residents, most all white, who were pressing us to close the kitchen—because "feeding people was only enabling their addictions"—I received and read minutes of their meeting prior. I reproduce a portion of them here, not to vilify but to edify. Truly. I often use them in teaching urban ministry courses. They are, in the truest sense, "classic," and ought to be part of a case study volume. Names have been deleted. To wit:

> Hi Conquistadors [remember, I'm not making this up]. The meeting was super. PLEASE FORWARD TO ANYONE YOU THINK MIGHT BE INTERESTED. (My email list is not very big.) For everyone who wasn't there: we've picked four projects to get started on. (And a secret one that can't be discussed via email . . . how very mysterious.)

> 1. *The Music Festival* Hopefully, this totally radical indie rock concert will be held next year in front of the train station—in tandem with tour de troit, already a successful Corktown event. XXX, XXXXX and XXXX will be leading the Music Festival Committee—and working with XXXX, who is heading up the annual tour de troit. She's thinking the after-event this year can be a mini-music fest, which will help make next year's big festival debut all the better...
>
> 2. *Team Bagley Market.* These folks will start organizing complaints against Bagley Market, as well as rogue acts of bad will. We hope to make their operation as difficult as possible until the day when we can afford to swoop in and buy them out to open our own specialty grocery. Would anyone like to lead this team?
>
> 3. *The Bermuda Triangle.* This includes (but is not limited to) activism to stop the free handouts in our neighborhood that facilitate the drugs, crime and general malcontent that thrives from St. Peters to the Train Station to the Mission on Michigan. XXXX and I are hoping to go talk to the people at the church next week and will give an update. We'll try being nice first...

To exegete this memo, you need to begin with "conquistadors," which of course is "only a joke," but a revealing one with respect to white Eurocentric imperial supremacy and particularly oblivious (or not so) to the cultural context of southwest Detroit (Mexican, Guatemalan, Salvadoran barrio). The other way in is through the pronouns, including the possessive ones. Who are "we"? And what, by whom, is claimed as "ours"? In the wake of the memo, I proposed that we have some conversations together about a different way to do things, about community and gentrification, but the use of the latter word was deemed "pejorative and offensive."

One element of the current neighborhood redevelopment is the proliferation of bars, brew pubs, and distilleries. I count seventeen bars on or adjacent to Michigan—seven of them new in the last couple of years. Some are so close that St. Peter's is required to sign off on their liquor licenses. It's ironic for those so concerned about enabling addictions. One distillery, funded by a $7 billion Parisian company, purports to be a local production and goes by the name, Our/Detroit Vodka, both appropriating "Detroit" literally as a brand and exercising the imperial "our."

The primary matter of note is that each of the agenda items has been or is being addressed. The park in front of the train station now has its own conservancy and hosts a totally indie rock festival as an annual event, along with a barbecue tent, and the starting line for the bike tour, plus an annual "corn hole" tournament. Roosevelt Park, long a home and hang out for homeless folk, had its benches officially removed to preempt loiterable rest. And one mid-November a police sweep carted off people's tents and lean-tos, kindly removing residents to shelters or if need be jail. The train station itself had been empty and abandoned for decades, stripped and windowless, a fascination for ruin porn urban spelunkers, and a perpetual set for movies—feature and indie zombie alike. Owned by real estate billionaire Matty Maroon, who also holds the Ambassador Bridge, it is now secured and commercial windows are going it.

To be frank, I was never a big fan of Bagley Market. It has had issues over the years. But rogue acts of bad will had never occurred to me. Our approach was to start a community garden across the street on church property. But now someone has swooped in to buy it; the upstairs residents are put out and the place is undergoing gut rehab. What specialty enterprise is about to move in remains to be seen.

As to the pivots of the Bermuda Triangle, Roosevelt Park is dealt with. If the other two are not openly for sale, they are at least viewed as marketable targets. I confess to wondering what the buyers might envision for us at St. Peter's. I suppose leveling the whole place and building condos from scratch to architecturally mirror "The Corner" across the street is one option. Another: perhaps our social justice beehive would become market rate offices and the church a performance space and night club. The sanctuary itself, with good acoustics, is deeply contemplative and beautiful. Built in the midst of the '29 crash (the most notorious previous burst of a financial bubble), it remains unfinished: walls of exposed brick do readily harken to that urban loft ambiance. The basement, preserving the linoleum, the stainless steel, and the worn woodwork, could be a restaurant—Manna Community Grill and Brew Pub.

But our guests? Those who come for food and warmth, for improvised community, for being treated with dignity and respect, who variously make the neighborhood home—they would be found elsewhere.

WHAT'S IN A NAME?

I used to serve as associate to a congregation in the Cass Corridor, somewhat north of Corktown. That was a neighborhood teeming with life and culture, single-room occupancy hotels, street life in parks and porches and projects, bars where Sixto Rodriguez regularly played. A place where they use to "kick out the jams." The church served the neighborhood, which poured daily in and out the front door. We had a senior center, a program for the developmentally disabled, youth basketball programing, and open meals. We were connected to the local school and were home to Michigan Welfare Rights. When they set up a tent city for homeless folks, it was next door to the church. We hosted the local community organization and founded a Housing Development Project.

Now the neighborhood has been rebranded as "Midtown." The SROs are most all gone, some converted to condos. The University Police, the largest private force in the city, patrols the community. The corporations and the medical center pay their employees to move in as renters or buyers, though the Cass Corridor Neighborhood Development Corporation still holds and rehabs buildings for fixed- and middle-income folks. At the church, there is still a worshiping community on Sundays and its programs are actually larger than ever, heavily funded by the state and the foundations—but many are located elsewhere, at a big facility in northwest Detroit. What is the role and responsibility of the church in community, specifically with respect to displacement?

Rebranding, this contrived changing of names, is a common and important aspect of gentrification. Do you call it Midtown or Cass Corridor? What do you remember? What do you forget?

Ironically, the Cass in Cass Corridor is Governor-cum-General Lewis Cass, who was Andrew Jackson's secretary of war during Indian removal, and among the largest land owners in Michigan (including 500 acres along the Detroit waterfront). He brought the indigenous community repeatedly to the council table for one last concession of land. In 1819 Chief Ogemawke intoned,

> *Your people trespass on our hunting grounds. You flock to our shores. Our waters grow warm. Our lands melt away like a cake of ice. Our possessions grow smaller and smaller. The warm wave of the white mane rolls in upon us and melts us away. Our women reproach us. Our children want homes. Shall we sell from under them the spot where they spread their blankets?*[10]

The heart of the corridor has been the intersection of Cass Avenue and Martin Luther King Drive. The name, "Cass Corridor," for all its untold irony, had been embraced by a community full of life.

---

10. Conot, *American Odyssey*, 25.

"Midtown," a moniker contrived by a foundation-funded non-profit, is a name that erases not just the sordid history of Governor Cass, but the remembrance of poor and black, Chinese and Indian people's business and street life. It is a name better suited to the stops of a rail line connecting downtown to the New Center area.

Names of neighborhood schools have likewise been changed by emergency management. The elected school board in exile has fought the gratuitous renaming of Finney High School to East English Village Academy (Finney was an abolitionist and East English Village is a another newly fabricated name), Barbara Jordan (the first African American congresswoman) to Palmer Park Academy; Ethelyn Crockett (African American doctor and wife of late congressman George Crockett) to Benjamin Carson Vo Tech (black Republican presidential candidate who argues that prison proves being gay is a choice).

A friend of mine struggled long and hard over whether to show her mother the published map by which the new white mayor (whether he is legitimate and truly elected is a whole other question) redesignates Mexicantown as "the Garment District." For a variety of reasons the earlier name had been struggled over (did it reflect the actual Latino diversidad?), but it was a name finally claimed with pride. In the thirties, 15,000 Detroiters (many of them native citizens) were "repatriated" back to Mexico on the nationwide depression premise that the Mexicans were taking our jobs. Most who survived returned home to Mexicantown. Now some of them live in the Garment District, named not necessarily for the bitter notion of border *maquiladoras*, but for newly arrived Detroit fashion start-ups. (See http://www.motheringjustice.org/mama-blog.)

SUBSIDIZED HOUSING IN CORKTOWN

Actually, if you look at demographic stats for the neighborhood, they would appear pretty diverse, but some boundaries are stark. The potato famine brought the huge influx of Irish to Detroit in the mid-nineteenth century. They were followed by Maltese and Mexican communities.

Corktown history buffs love to tell the story, and rightly so, of the struggle to save the neighborhood from the leveling hand of urban renewal. Postwar, two neighborhoods were chosen as "blighted" and for destruction. Then as now, *blight* was a slippery term whose meaning mostly suited the purposes of those who wanted the land. Hastings Street (Black Bottom/

Paradise Valley with enormous cultural assets and vitality) was poor and African American; Corktown was two-thirds Maltese and Mexican. People in Corktown organized, signed petitions, did neighborhood clean-ups, improved their homes, and went to City Council hearings. Father John Mangrum, one of my predecessors at St. Peter's, spoke and wrote against the clearing. He did not mince words: "Destroy families, tear up homes, and supplant them with questionable business development and the wrath of God will fall on this city." But the council voted unanimously to clear 129 acres between Michigan and Fort Street.

Rebuilt housing promised for 140 displaced families never materialized. Light industry filled the space, as was the city's plan, except for a three-block stretch, a bufferland along Bagley that remained vacant for a quarter century. I remember walking across it regularly. You could flush pheasants up from the deep grass and I still have a photo of the path cross at its center where two diagonal short cuts intersected. Eventually a group of Corktown neighbors, spearheaded by Shirley Beaupre, now of blessed memory, decided that subsidized housing should be built there. In 1985 they accomplished the low and moderate income project, called Clem Kern Gardens after Corktown's other activist priest. Now surrounded by an iron grate fence, it never served the Mexican community and today is virtually all black. But hence the good diversity stats.

You want my guess? The Farmington Hills speculators have noticed its location and value. Perhaps the management company has received a cold call. I bet the iron fence comes down if it's converted to condominiums. A new name is probably in the works too.

Meanwhile, there is still subsidized housing in Corktown, but it's of a very different sort. A number of corporations (Quicken Loans, DTE, the Detroit Medical Center, Blue Cross/Blue Shield) pay their employees to move into Downtown, Midtown, Corktown, and other select neighborhoods. Quicken, which aggressively denies selling predatory loans but which profited enormously from the mortgage crisis in Detroit, recently built a multimillion-dollar fiber optic data storage site in the neighborhood. And pays its workers $20K in forgivable loans to buy a house in Corktown, or $2,500 to rent. Full disclosure: this is an issue for us at St. Peter's because we have a house that we now rent as a two flat and the first person to apply for it was from Quicken. We had to decide whether we would participate in the program or not and to think through a policy. We do consider it a subsidy, not one enabling poor folks to live in mixed income neighborhoods, but one for corporate employees, artificially altering the market, effectively raising rents and values, and forcing poorer folks out. So we have declined officially and publicly to participate.

Michigan Avenue business start-ups are subsidized too. A number, including one of the distilleries, have gotten grants that I believe come from the earmark for the Tiger Stadium site. A bagel shop, great place, good coffee, nice folks, dedicated localists, got $50K. I'll bet Gold Cash Gold too.

DISPLACEMENT, RACE, AND THE G-WORD

The term *gentrification* originated in England where the landed gentry were moving back into London neighborhoods and displacing the poor and working-class residents. It's an urban economic process where depressed land values draw investment that changes those values (taxes, rents, and costs), driving people out. But it is also where driving people out changes land values. Those who take umbrage at use of the term in this neighborhood constantly assert that no one is being displaced.

Further downtown, but toward Corktown, there is an apartment building which has been renamed the Albert, after its famous architect, Albert Kahn. Residents were evicted and a major rehab and condominiumization was undertaken. This is happening many places near the city center where vacancy rates are now less than 5 percent. As conversion became complete a promotional video, geared to young people, was produced. It was largely an advertisement for downtown and portrayed the vitality and resources of city living. "It's our generation's turn now," it proclaimed. Read the pronouns again. Visuals were full of marble countertops, strip lighting, and hardwood floors—and mostly white folks crooning about this place, this time. On YouTube and Facebook it generated lots of hits, including much ire and unanticipated pushback. Kind of the video equivalent of the conquistador memo. Before they could pull it down, brilliant guerilla filmmaker Kate Levy snatched it off public media and mashed it up with interviews she had done with the mostly black residents in walkers and wheelchairs telling of their struggles to remain in the building or have some of the apartments reserved for them. It's very moving. (See http://katelevy.virb.com/detroit-videos.)

This was not a Dan Gilbert/Quicken building, but he had one just like it next door—one of his sixty downtown properties bought at fire sale prices.

A few months ago, Nolan Finley, an opinion editor at *The Detroit News*, who has been an unabashed supporter of emergency management, new white "Mayor" Mike Duggan, Detroit bankruptcy, and water shutoffs, wrote a surprising lament about downtown called "Where are the Black People?" He'd suddenly noticed their absence from upscale venues and downtown festivals.

> It's a clear red flag when you can sit in a hot new downtown restaurant and nine out of 10 tables are filled with white diners, a proportion almost exactly opposite of the city's racial make-up.... It should stop us in our tracks—as it did me the other day—when a group of 50 young professionals being groomed for future leadership shows up to hear advice from a senior executive, and there's only one Black member among them.

Why African Americans hadn't done the same thing as the white suburban creatives seizing opportunity in Detroit seemed a mystery to him. But he was pretty sure it wasn't about racism and he thought it outright ridiculous to say it was about gentrification.

Not everyone is averse to the g-word. Former economic czar George Jackson Jr., who recently resigned as head of the Detroit Economic Growth Corporation, named it just "one of the costs of progress." Last year he told a Grosse Pointe audience, "When I look at this city's tax base, I say bring on more gentrification . . . I'm sorry, but, I mean, bring it on." Emergency management, DEGC, and mayoral policies effectively encourage it.

A year ago Spike Lee let loose his notorious rant about gentrification in Bedford Stuyvesant—police protection, city services, name changes, access to schools, and cultural disrespect all figured in. Yet there are big differences between Detroit gentrification and that same process in Brooklyn or Chicago where land values, population density, and market centers do create intense competition and conspire rapid displacement. To understand gentrification in Detroit involves panning back to the bigger picture of displacement in the city as a whole.

MOVING PEOPLE OUT

The reduction of the city's population from 2 million in the fifties to maybe 700,000 at present happened in waves over time. Nearly all were motivated or mediated by race as a matter of public and economic policy. Long before the 1967 rebellion, white flight was well organized. The suburbs were created postwar by guaranteed loans from the VA and Federal Housing Authority (FHA) that were only available for new housing and only for whites. Restrictive covenants (explicitly forbidding sale to blacks) built into title deeds were legally enforceable until the mid-fifties and functioned de facto thereafter. Guns and baseball bats backed them up. When housing discrimination was made technically illegal, banks devised "redlining" policies to restrict mortgage and loan credit from black neighborhoods, which were "not good investments," but offered them freely in white ones.

Disinvestment from the city was best signaled by the invention of the shopping mall, essentially by J. L. Hudsons—the first one in the US, erected just north of Eight Mile Road. Eventually Hudsons abandoned their downtown facility, which sat as a ghostly hulk until it was famously imploded. The auto companies moved headquarters or plants to the suburbs, even before they discovered the south and south of the border. Interstate expressways that decimated, divided, and displaced communities of color also enabled whites to move, but drive back into the city for their blue- and white-collar jobs.

There was good money to be made in moving white people. Real estate companies developed "blockbusting," a practice of controlling the line between the black and white communities. They would move one black family into a block and then send postcards to all the other houses on the block: "We've sold a home on your street; if you might also be interested in selling please call . . . ." Racial and economic fears were fused and people indeed sold quickly. I went to Cooley High School in the sixties and I saw those postcards on Ardmore Street. Cheap homes invited absentee landlords and speculators extracting rent without maintaining properties. Meanwhile, real estate developers were busy throwing up homes and strip malls, inventing suburban sprawl.

White flight, industrial flight, job flight, and capital flight were engineered, and did indeed strip the city's tax base, devalue its land, impoverish its people, and corrupt its housing stock.

Fast forward to the most recent waves of population loss, equally driven by race. The financial crisis and depression of 2007 were constructed on financial instruments that bundled sub-prime mortgages into marketable securities. Predatory loans had actually been targeted and disproportionately sold in black communities. People who once owned their homes outright found themselves facing impossible balloon payments, foreclosure, and eviction. Now the city, once with the largest number of homeowners in the nation, has become the city with the largest number of foreclosures. The whole thing was actually illegal, but the banks got bailed out. And then their loans (not the current value of the home they took back but the full value of the original loan) were covered by Fannie Mae and Freddie Mac. Now if they sat on the house, refusing to sell, and it burned mysteriously, they got the insurance settlement as well. Sounds like triple dipping to me. It was a massive financial extraction that further wasted black neighborhoods in Detroit.

At the last census there was a scramble to count homeless folks and find a million people in Detroit, but it turned out we could only locate 713,000. Geez, what happened to all those people? Expelled? Displaced? Irresponsible borrowers consigned to the economic darkness.

And here is where the Detroit gentrification narrative diverges from Chicago or Bed Stuy. Now a city with 139 square miles has over forty square miles in vacant land, many in small parcels. So infrastructure for the big space and twice the people. A certain logic dictates what Mayor Bing called downsizing. How to do that in a way that serves all residents, especially the least and the poorest?

There is a one-inch thick book of maps called *Detroit Future City*, a study funded by foundations. It's not a democratically accountable city planning document, but Mayor Duggan's chief planner once called it his new bible. It makes not a single mention of race, or racial distribution in the city, but it suggests neighborhoods that have a future and will receive infrastructure and support, and others whose future is to become green space or water retention areas. This also means clearing land into large tracts that can be developed later or sooner. What about the folks who still live in those areas, who have hung in and tried to hold community in a deteriorating neighborhood, planting gardens in the shards? Are they getting eminent domain payments for their properties?

No. But here is how they can be driven out: withdraw city services. Close the neighborhood schools and let them decay before your eyes. Churches can be withdrawn too. (Before the last round of church closings the cardinal sat down with the mayor to find out which neighborhoods had no future.) When precincts go, crime increases intolerably. There is a history in Detroit of using drug traffic concentration to clear neighborhoods slated for redevelopment. Think Brush Park, State Fair Grounds, Detroit Airport. If you turn off hydrants and withdraw or distance firehouses, smoke or fire can do the same thing. Years ago in Poletown arson was funded by demolition contractors paying kids to set blazes—it being easier to haul off a burned out hulk half carried away on the wind. But the winds of fear and smoke also carry people off.

Residential water can be shut off. That drives out renters first. Last year there were 33,000. With spring at hand the shutoff season is about to resume with 36,000 homes slated, 3,000 per week. This year add 8,000 homes whose valve boxes will be removed from the property. These are civil disobedients who have claimed water as a human right, but whom the city labels as thieves. Moreover, water bills are now attached as liens to tax bills, so home owners can be foreclosed for being in arears. Next week 65,000 homes in Detroit will go into tax foreclosure—37,000 of them are occupied. Perhaps 100 thousand poor and black folks sent packing from their inconvenient neighborhoods. Their properties will go the largest landlord in the city: the Detroit Land Bank. (See http://www.theatlantic.com/business/archive/2014/10/one-fifth-of-detroits-population-could-lose-their-homes/381694/.)

Isn't there money to keep people in their homes? There is: upwards of $400 million in federal funds designated for Hardest Hit Homeowners. But it's not being released by the governor. Well, a third of it has been released for demolition and blight removal. The Detroit Blight Removal Authority is headed by Bill Pulte, grandson of the largest homebuilder in the country, based in Bloomfield Hills. The Detroit Blight Task Force, which did the mapping of neighborhoods and the structures to be demolished, is headed by Dan Gilbert—owner of sixty downtown buildings—who aggressively denies selling sub-prime mortgages in Detroit. Both have vested interests which profit from the clearing of black and poor neighborhoods in Detroit.

Here we come close to the variety of gentrification in Detroit. There are increasingly two Detroits. One growing, largely white, and monied— neighborhoods along the riverfront and the Woodward corridor, as well as a few others along the spoke streets of the city. The other is poor and black and increasingly wiped out. The one is privileged, with resources public and private. Wealth from the other is squeezed as extraction. Displacement in the latter benefits the former in resources, infrastructure, and land value.

Think about it: the marketable value of St. Peter's corner goes up not just because of development across the street, but because of the clearing of land and expelling of people from other neighborhoods. The market, as they say, becomes more focused. We are privileged by their loss. Does it have to be so?

OUR CONFESSION

If you live in the Catholic Worker neighborhood and feel judged, even convicted, by this story and you are still reading, then you are the very person I am hoping would read. If you live or work or worship in the Catholic Worker neighborhood and are happily reading along because, like me, you could feel justified by this story, then you too are one I am hoping would read. If you live in a part of the city and have qualms about your location, if you live in the suburbs and know the real history of how you got there and you support the struggles of people in Detroit, if you reside in a portion of the city under assault as blighted and without future, even if you are a public official, or a private one for that matter, tracking the narratives about gentrification and having a hand in public policy—then you are among those I've been hoping would read this.

My own confession is that I live in a two-block stretch of southwest Detroit that is in danger of becoming a white enclave. When our family moved here more than twenty years ago it was the aging rear guard of an eastern European neighborhood that since has become majority Latino—Mexican and Guatemalan. At one point there were seventeen connected households of white families, part of the extended Catholic Worker activist community. We had a common life together on our block, but not much relationship to our neighbors. Notice the pronouns. I am confessing them.

When it came time for all our children to begin high school, a number of our community moved out of the city, largely for the sake of education. Our family stayed on the block, but our girls went to an excellent Catholic high school in Farmington Hills. This was during the first state takeover of the public schools at the turn of the century by the Engler administration—done in order to control, direct, and extract the nearly one billion dollars in bond money for school reconstruction, but it also was also the beginning of a process of dismantling public education in Detroit. To facilitate that a campaign by New Detroit and others denigrating DPS was developed, and I suppose we bought the mainstream narrative. To cut ourselves some grace, this was also a period in which our family was coping with a medical crisis, so we were not much in a position to engage the struggle around public education, but neither were we invested in it as parents.

Our family was privileged to have our daughters well educated. They are still on the block and in the community engaging the city's movement struggles for justice. I'm proud of them. In fact a number of the young people who moved away are coming home to our street, rerooting. As that happens (we are now much more connected in community with neighbors on the block) and as other young white folks with good urban politics are likewise drawn to the neighborhood, we are forced to be asking ourselves: how do we keep from gentrifying our own street? We slow new moves. And we keep this confessional, self-critical question before our faces and our hearts.

Gentrification for some is a calculated strategy. But for others, much like white supremacy and privilege, it operates in a blissful self-ignorance. "What water?" says the fish. Both must be named to be seen, and often painfully so. Both must be confessed. I'd be glad if this story was part of that confession.

The questions remain. Can we have a real conversation about gentrification in Detroit? Here in St. Peter's parish, in the Catholic Worker neighborhood? Not another panel discussion with questions controlled on cards or tweets, but the sit-down one I proposed, though not well perhaps, when the conquistador memo first came out? I can say that St. Peter's would be willing to host it. Could we honor the history and struggle of the neighborhood and city, not as ironic kitsch nostalgia, but as a way of joining a living struggle for justice now going on? Is gentrification just a relentless process that grinds on oblivious of human lives, or can it be creatively resisted and altered inside and out? Can a neighborhood be consciously and truly mixed income, including street people, or is there no alternative to apartheid security? What would we have to slow or stop, what encourage and support? Could the "our" in our neighborhood be not exclusionary, but wide and universal? Whose city? Our city! Whose neighborhood? Our neighborhood! Whose community? Our beloved community!

2015

For Grace Boggs, at one hundred

RADICAL DISCIPLESHIP, A BLOG PARTNERING WORD AND
WORLD AND BARTIMEAUS COOPERATIVE MINISTRIES

Hope—a feathered thing?
      Less perched than lifting off with raptor wings
      spanning a community of roots
      in their woven reach for earth
Hope, she says in quotes, is a revolution of values,
      one with the arcing bend of this beloved universe,
      initiated like a communal intervention:
      some twelve-step plan against the monkey-backed fuel-fed
      addictions of consumer culture, this sweet and sore planet's woe.
      Let others simply live
Hope is resistance, a history of conscience told
      against the saving narratives or emergency and disaster management
      where do we place our learning when they dismantle education?
Imagine: making hay of industrial demise;
      Start with dirt, beneath the nails of a calloused common hand.
      Ask what time? What place?
As a discipline to practice,
hope is akin to marriage or friendship
      honored unbreakably in the struggle's long haul:
      the political, beloved,

is personal, dear comrade.
>   Find it in economy as neighborhood
>   a bartered thing that keeps coming round
>   this uncommodifiable but still recirculatable gift
>   passed like eggs, tomatoes, or tamales down the block
>   hosed like water, one house to the next
>   radioed like pirate news, ciphers on the wind

Hope is an undocumented Spirit.
>   She crosses the borderland of empires' collapse
>   to another world possible, buried beneath extraction, expulsion
>   a new city happening, the art of the found, the noticed, the embraced
>   this cultural economy of gift
>   our human contradictions notwithstanding
>   the very dialectics of grace . . .

2015

A Cemetery for Buried Streams

On the Edge, "A Small Covenant of Land and Waters," Summer 2015

Come summer then through fall, we used to take our daughters for regular walks in Elmwood Cemetery on the near east side of Detroit. A favorite photo has them looking up there in sun, caught by delight. This European burial ground is the last surviving bit of pre-Columbian terrain in the city. All the remaining earth has been cleared and graded and leveled first as farmland, then paved as urban built environment. This is not to say it's old growth forest (any of that wood is long hauled off and the subsequent transplants tended into a canopy of stately beauties), but the land has rocky outcrops, ridges, rills, and a stream that emerges from underground to pool before slipping back beneath the street toward the river.

That stream, first called Parents Creek, had a name change in 1763 when Pontiac's warriors were encamped there. Risen up against the British and laying siege to Fort Detroit, the Odawa were attacked, though not surprised, by 250 troops. The stream ran red with British blood, and is remembered since as Bloody Run.

There are many such streams shedding water to the great river. Five years ago during the US Social Forum in Detroit, environment justice activists walked the route of the Savoyard Creek, which, encased in a brick tomb, still carries rainwater run-off, even flowing under the Buhl building and by the Penobscot "Temple of Finance" all beneath the streets of downtown

Detroit. The activists made puppets of creatures past and present, then undertook a festive procession at street level following the ghostwaters, as they called them. Sturgeon and trout, birds and bugs swarmed the streets in a liturgy of memory, celebration, and resistance.

Detroit is a cemetery for buried creeks, some with living water still. In Southwest there is buried stream called Baby Creek, or in the French, Bau Bee, running from the Spring Wells area of Delray. On the east side, my friend keeps a boat at the foot of Meadow Brook Road. Also north and east, Connor's Creek flows under the I-94 Ford Freeway which rises from the cement ditch at the golf course to get over its underground run.

Recently and incidentally these have been invoked in the Detroit water struggle. Those ridiculing water as a human right are not above saying, "Yes, it's your right. Take your bucket down to the creek and draw what you want." Charity Hicks, urban agriculturalist and water warrior now of blessed memory responded, "Really? Show me the creek!"

Sometimes when I'm watering the garden at St. Peter's, I think of the stream, variously called Campau's Creek, then Gabacier's, then May's, which flowed just a block or so south across Trumbull Avenue. Where its route approaches the river it was covered by the Michigan Central Station and its bed used for a rail line.

We garden in a dozen raised beds because the soil around St. Peter's tests high for lead. We began Manna Community Garden six or seven years ago when there was drug activity kitty-corner from the church. Gardening is a way of reclaiming social space and building community, as much as it is about growing our own food. The project has always been a collaboration between the church, the Catholic Worker soup kitchen (Manna Community Meal), and our neighbors.

Manna is a Hebrew word that means "what is it"? It's the flaky "bread," found on the ground, which the Israelites lived on in the wilderness after they walked out of Egypt. The wilderness sojourn was a time of unlearning empire, so manna was a lesson and a test. Imperial economy is one of domination and extraction—taking, storing, and hoarding. The Hebrew slaves, in fact, were making bricks for the building of granary storage facilities. That's empire in a nutshell. By contrast, Manna economy is one of gift, of sharing, of sufficiency. It means living in accord with the land and not collecting more than one's need for the day. If an Israelite tried to store up extra manna, it rotted and stank. "Give us this day our daily bread" means no one has more than they need and everyone has enough. It must have been an important lesson because the only things kept in the ark of the covenant were the stone tablets of the law and a jar of manna—just enough to remember.

Manna Community Garden enjoys a good bit of "street harvest." In some community gardens that can be a problem (there are over 430 of them in the city, among the 1,386 registered plots), but we're cool with it, even happy for it. As the harvest comes in we also bring the fruits and roots and leaves to the altar, where they join with the gifts of Eucharist. At the end of the service congregants and guests take what they need. The altar names the gift and serves as a point of redistribution.

A few weeks ago, after the hot crops went in, we made a Sunday morning procession to the beds for our garden blessing. We sang, poured water upon it, and remade our covenant. Hear these words:

> *By and through Manna Community Garden, we renew ourselves in God's covenant with all creation. In it we pledge ourselves to help protect this fragile and finite earth. We stand together against all threats to this place and to the great community of life. As followers of Jesus we commit ourselves anew to one another, to our neighbors, and to the growing among us of justice and community. May we walk as lightly upon this riverbank land as did the Anishinaabe peoples, the Huron, the Odawa. We honor the air, the waters, and even the earth as a commons which must neither be stolen nor poisoned. So what we grow, what we receive from this good earth, we give and share at common tables. We do so partnering with worms and water, sun and air, with living soil beneath us, and all the forces of life. Together we pledge to notice beauty in our city and God's creation: the opening leaf, the sunrise and sunset, flowers and fruit, rainbows arching high, the power of starlight, the faces of one another on the street, and all forms of life among whom we live. Here we listen to the "music of the universe"—the sound of water falling to earth, trees bending in the wind, the world waking and warming to morning sun. We remember to reverence all that God has created. Let this garden bless us and bless our community.*

Amen. So be it.

2015

From *Wahnabeezee* to PenskeLand: the Desecration of Detroit's Belle Isle

DETROITERS RESISTING EMERGENCY MANAGEMENT, 2015

If you are a Detroiter stopping at the gatehouse to pay the fee or show your state-issued recreational pass (or even if you are watching events from afar), know this: Detroit never leased Belle Isle, its island park, to the state of Michigan. City Council refused that deal. A lease was signed by Emergency Manager Kevyn Orr, whose authority has still not been constitutionally tested in federal court. Think of it this way: through his own appointee it was leased to the state by Governor Snyder.

An emergency manager, by the way, is not a financial manager, as you might assume. He has vested in himself all the powers of government and more. He can, we are told, write laws, repeal ordinances, set budgets, privatize departments, sell assets, break contracts (union and otherwise), file for municipal bankruptcy, rewrite the charter, and dissolve the city government. Three-quarters of all black elected officials in Michigan have been replaced by emergency managers. It's a long back story. But you should know at least that much.

As to the park, improvements are underway to bring it back to the glory days of the 1950s. It is being remodeled to comport with a downtown made safe for white people, whose numbers grow. Detroit is the last remaining major city in the nation with a black majority. But for how long?

BELLE ISLE LOVES

OK, I'm a white person. I truly love Belle Isle and want to love it still. Last week I sat at one of its plank tables with a pint of shrimp creole from the Louisiana on Gratiot, and thought of my history here. I do have the memories from the fifties and sixties of picnics and free band concerts near the carillon and of watching the model power boats cruise the cement pond along the south bank. My daughters could name their own childhood recollections, some involving playscapes, the giant slide (first in my arms then solo), and a llama who ate a pacifier dropped into its pen by the little girl looking down from the overhead boardwalk of the children's zoo. Or more recently, pulling up an invasive species, *phragmites*, by the root.

More of my own and deeper still. In 1981 when I was struggling over ordination, I walked the island with a friend, this mendicant nonviolent activist. In the midst of conversation, he turned to me and said, "Well, Bill, what's it going to be, Jesus or the church?" Have a nice Zen whack. I still don't want to believe the choice must be that sharp, but I keep the question before me to this day.

Two years ago I did a baptism in the river. As St. Peter's congregants waded in along the north beach bearing an infant, we were mindful that this water runs to the ocean and so is connected directly to all the waters of earth. It is a common gift of grace.

I've also done weddings on the island, one by the lighthouse on the east point that involved kites that broke free of their strings in the wind. Another was supposed to be held in the formal gardens by the conservatory, but turned out to coincide with a massive funk festival so crowded that the cops closed the bridge. I pulled my pastoral credentials and finally got waved in, but the couple and their crowd couldn't get through. My call from a pay phone located them at the "after party," now already in full swing at a Mexicantown bar. When I got there I suggested that the wedding party go down to Riverside Park for the ceremonials, but it was jammed with families who couldn't get onto the island either. When I asked permission to use the front lawn of the post office that serves the passing freighters, they said, "How about on the mail boat? We're about to make a delivery." Promises were on the lawn, but we took the ride. Moving full speed, hull pressed to hull, they hoisted mail up and down in a bucket.

I myself made a proposal of marriage on a bridge by the casino, so-called. And I've fallen in love on the island. I could show you a spot where the sun shone down on the swan boats, now long gone. For that matter, I've not fallen in love on the island too. A dear and beloved friend once walking with me along the canal behind the aquarium made a forthright declaration of love. But my own heart had to leave it there unrequited.

My partner Jeanie, now of blessed memory, had her bachelorette "shower" after midnight beneath a full moon *in* the Scott Fountain. There was wine and many a blessing, I'm told. James Scott, by the way, a notorious and hot-tempered gambler at the turn of the century, left the city his entire fortune for building a monument to himself. The council balked. Then relented and built a fountain. Lift a toast to James.

Also in the eighties I played softball in the Detroit Athletic League on the island's play field. Though we had our own ringers, the firemen and the policemen consistently kicked our butts. No mind. I played third base and I swear every game I had a view of the full moon rising and the freighters slipping by. Need I say that for me, as for many, this isle has been holy ground?

DEEP HISTORIES

There is a pictorial history of the park, full of quaint interesting facts, which is commended and drawn upon here (Rodriguez and Featherstone, *Detroit's Belle Isle*, Arcadia, 2003). Such histories, however, like all, are shaped by who owns the camera and where they stand to shoot. It's necessary to read between the pics, or peer outside the frame, in my view. I confess to having a perspective. I pray I stand somewhere to rehearse a little island history, one falling along the fault lines of race and class, of the public and private.

From beginning to end, there is no city here without the river. Its fate and form and function are all tied to the passing waters. Places have names and names bear history. The Huron, the Ojibwa, and Odawa called this stretch *Wawiatonong*, "where the river goes round." It was for them a place of gathering. They tread lightly on its banks and in accord with all its creatures.

One clan of relations in those days were the sturgeon who ranged far, from watershed to watershed, through the river. Ancient beings who preceded the dinosaurs in North America, they would reach eight feet in length and could weigh in at three hundred pounds. Indigenous communities gratefully caught them for meat and buried their bones as honored relatives, never burning them. Europeans eventually harvested the fish *en masse*, only for their swim bladder, which figured in the distillation of alcohol. In the Midwest, their corpses piled up like cordwood. Winona LaDuke says, "Their destruction was so intense, you could think of sturgeon as the buffalo of the aquatic ecosystem." (*Recovering the Sacred*, South End, 2005.) Or even, I suppose, the beaver.

The Europeans called the river *d'Etroit*, "the straight," and it was for them a channel for transport of firs, then timber, coal, and ores. It was defended with forts and came to mark a border between nations. Eventually it washed their machines and carried off their petrochemical wastes.

The island also had names and changes, each marking a moment. In Anishinaabe it was first *Wahnabeezee*, "Swan Island," then Snake Island, Hog Island, and finally Belle Isle. When the French first passed through coming down from the north, they came upon a stone formation, vaguely human, on the river bank that was certainly a sacred gathering place. There was evidence of gifts left. Regarding it as a heathen idol, the two priests in the delegation broke it to bits with a "consecrated axe." Here the stories diverge. A European account is that the stones were borne to the middle of the river and sunk. Indigenous memory says that they were found or recovered and the shattered pieces borne to the island where the shards transformed into an infestation of snakes.

The snakes are an undisputed matter of fact. They inhabited the island marshes.

To suppress them and to keep their livestock safe from marauding wolves, the settlers grazed their pigs on what had now become "Hog Island," *Isle aux Cochons*. Livestock signals that the French, somewhat akin to the indigenous communities, held the island to be a "commons," shared by all. The Odawa village was then set where the bridge now lands. It was not until 1763, following Pontiac's rebellion and hence for military reasons, that King George III authorized from afar (shades of Governor Snyder) that it could be deeded into private hands. Lt. George McDonald paid five barrels of rum and a belt of Wampum for the island. It was subsequently named Belle Isle in honor of beauty and perhaps a family member.

FAULT LINES OF RACE AND CLASS

It would be a hundred years before it was purchased by the city of Detroit for $200,000 to make of it a city park, freed to be the commons once again. The project was designed and championed by Frederick Law

Olmstead, more notorious for his design of New York's Central Park. (Actually he threw up his hands and walked away from Belle Isle in exasperation.) It was contested matter. Rich people had no interest in a commons for ordinary folk, but were then pushing instead for development of Grand Boulevard, a greenway around the city, practically a private park serving their big homes. Industrialists saw the island as the easiest way for bridging to Canada and featured a rail yard on its land between. Moreover, the placement of the intake for the new water works on the park would legally limit industrial development on the river for six miles upstream. As it was, the city's waterfront was otherwise completely given over to industry, inaccessible to citizens. When the plan went forward it was a humanizing victory for workers. And in the midst of an early depression, it was also a labor-intensive public works project to boot: picture the canal system and the lakes being dug by hand with pick and shovel.

In the years that followed half the fun was the boat ride to the island docking near the big bathhouse at the western tip. For six cents you could ride back and forth all day. When the first bridge was built it began from the foot of the boulevard with Electric Park, a ferris-wheeled amusement park on both sides. That bridge, which pivoted at the center to allow boat traffic, caught fire and burned beyond repair. Its remains lie still at the bottom of the river.

The current bridge, the McArthur, was completed in 1923, and brought an end to Electric Park. As the Great Depression loomed, shanty town Hoovervilles sprang up and people froze to death on the streets of Detroit. Downriver the Hunger Marchers were met by Ford with fire hoses and guns at the Miller Street Bridge. Five people were killed and many more wounded. By 1935, jumping from the Belle Isle Bridge, eighty-seven people had committed suicide. Though no great drop, the icy water and strong current made it deadly nonetheless. All these are wounds the island carries and bears.

Perhaps the deepest wound, and one most pertinent to the present moment, was the race riot of 1943, which began on the island. In the wake of the Great Migration and in a city otherwise clearly segregated Belle Isle was the one place black and white folk did freely mingle. Little wonder it was the flash point.

The story bears telling in detail and the context is important. First say the atmosphere was charged with racism. Father Coughlin, who practically invented hate radio in Detroit, preached a running mix of anti-Semitic, anti-communist, white supremacy. It was in the air and fouled the wind.

With respect to housing there were two clearly circumscribed neighborhoods for Negroes—Black Bottom, named for the for the dark soil of its low land, including Hastings Street and Paradise Valley—being the one on the near east side. With populations rising as driven by the war effort in Detroit's Arsenal of Democracy, the federal government built two public housing projects, one for white folks and another, Sojourner Truth Homes, for blacks. However, in 1942, when time came to move in, white neighbors adjacent rose up with pickets to block the way of the first fourteen families. A small riot ensued. But the feds held firm. The archdiocese ordered Coughlin off the air.

In the plants black folk were consigned to the foundry and the most dangerous or back-breaking work—and at the lowest pay. Just months prior at the Packard plant, now one of Detroit's most famous ruins, three black workers were promoted on the basis of seniority and 25,000 white defense workers walked out. Outside circling the factory were vehicles with loudspeakers blaring, "Better for Hitler and Hirohito to win the war than to work next to a nigger." Here the powers acceded. (Conot, *American Odyssey*, Wayne State, 1986.)

You could see it coming. *Life* magazine did. In an issue on the city they wrote, "Detroit is Dynamite. It could blow up Hitler, or it could blow up the U.S."

It was a 90 degree day in June of 1943 (actually the weekend of "Juneteenth," when African Americans celebrate news of the Emancipation Proclamation and Union victory finally reaching slaves in Texas—June 19, 1865). Tempers were flaring on the crowded island. Incidents of racial conflict were breaking out. In the process, however, the police searched vehicles and possessions of black folks, but not whites. As evening fell and people headed home, the bridge was a bottleneck, packed with departing car and foot traffic. Things jumped off there in a bloody brawl, exacerbated by hundreds of white sailors pouring out of the new naval armory at the foot of the bridge.

Among those fleeing, two different rumors spread throughout the city. In the white neighborhoods it was reported that Negroes had raped a white woman on the island. In the black community, including a bar on Hastings Street, news was spread that sailors had thrown a black woman and her baby off the bridge.

As Victoria Wolcott has written, "The rights of Black families to use Belle Isle unmolested was at stake, and the riot was, in part, a claiming of public recreational space in the city." (*Race, Riots, and Roller* Coasters, University of Pennsylvania, 2012.)

In the ensuing violence that broke out all over the city, the actions of Detroit's all-white police force were key. In white communities they relied on verbal persuasion or stood by watching assaults; whereas in black communities they employed nightsticks and guns. Police closed Brush Street and redirected African American drivers coming north right into the white mobs on Woodward, where cars were overturned and drivers beaten.

The NAACP report or the riot, backed with careful affidavits, was written by Thurgood Marshall. Thirty-five people died. Of the seventeen killed by police, all were black. There were 675 serious injuries and some 1,900 arrests (85 percent of those being black folks).[11]

The 2,500 National Guard troops which Roosevelt sent to Detroit made Belle Isle their base from which to quell the riot.

Just a footnote. When the 1967 rebellion broke out, the island was once again closed for fear and memory, and the old bath house then used as a holding cell for those arrested. Its makeshift arrangements made it look like a prisoner of war camp.

For the decades to follow the police force continued to function in the black community as a white occupation army. In the sixties a unit called STRESS (Stop The Robberies Enjoy Safe Streets) would use decoys to set up purse snatchings, then shoot fleeing black youth. Did their lives matter? Their wounds and deaths, to be sure, were not captured by iPhones or squad car cameras. Upon election, Coleman Alexander Young shut that unit down and integrated the police force.

TURNING UNDER SAFE AND SACRED GROUND

For the last forty years the park has been a beloved and racially safe space for black Detroiters. This is not to say there hasn't been crime or violence. This period includes the Reagan-era dump of crack cocaine into the cities and so passes through the years when Detroit was known as Murder City for its sad per capita record. The island was only a partial escape from these realities.

---

11. NAACP report in Hendrickson, *Detroit Perspectives*.

Yet they are also the days of concerts, walkers and joggers, swimming in the river, and many many family reunions. For Juneteenth weekend, pavilions are reserved long in advance. Whole clans descend from near and far donning printed T-shirts. Barbeque smoke wafts like sweet fog. Family trees are traced and the old stories rehearsed.

There are hidden histories which should be known and told. Rhonda Anderson, activist in the environmental justice movement, reports being shown a "healing tree" on the island. It was big willow near the east end fishing pier. She was told to go to the tree, and tell it your need. Then leave a gift of some sort. Over the years she did so many times, sitting and talking with the tree. Sometimes she buried a gift, but eventually took to pressing a coin into its bark. She would see evidence of others leaving offerings as well. One day a man approached as she sat and said, "Ah, you know about the trees." He told her there were actually three of them planted by his congregation along that stretch. It was the community founded by Prophet Jones, a charismatic preacher in a tradition that fused black nationalism with fiery Pentecostalism. Since their heyday included the forties I can't help but wonder if these plantings were a healing response to the '43 riot.

Last year she came and the tree was gone. It had suffered visible storm damage and the DNR took it down. In fact, all three of them. She spoke to a ranger at the nature center who said, "Oh, if we'd only known, we could have saved it!" That's the deal. You have to know the story, the layered meanings of a place. Sacred trees, like sacred rocks, may not speak for themselves, but their destruction can turn to curses.

Another story kin to it. For the twentieth anniversary of Earth Day in 1990 the EPA instituted a national day of tree planting. Working at the time with SOSAD (the anti-violence project called Save Our Sons And Daughters), Jimmy Boggs, himself a labor and community activist in Detroit, suggested connecting the day to a remembrance of the young people who had been killed by gun violence. There were several planting sites, but the big one was on Belle Isle. Not far from the casino, several hundred trees went in with names and ceremony and song. Shea Howell, who tells the story, reports that in the years that followed a lovely grove was beginning to form. Then came the improvements for the Grand Prix race and they were unceremoniously plowed under to make room for cement.

Mindy Fullilove, a professor of public health at Columbia who is also a doctor and psychiatrist, has written a book about black communities cleared by urban renewal. Most of her study focuses on Philadelphia and Pittsburgh, but the destruction of Hastings Street and Paradise Valley for the building of the I-75 expressway is poetically included. She argues that the clearing of neighborhoods, even ghettoes as it were, vibrant with community and culture, has a collective physical and psychological impact much like what happens to plants when they are uprooted. Her book is called *Root Shock* (Random House, 2009).

Detroit is currently being physically reconfigured by corporate and non-profit design. Though not an official planning document, *Detroit Future City* maps and identifies certain neighborhoods, like those along the river and the Woodward Corridor, which will be privileged with resources, infrastructure, and subsidies. Other neighborhoods, whose future is to be greenspace or water catchment areas, more patiently awaiting redevelopment, will be denied resources. Well, demolition resources can be found there, much of it taken from federal funds designated to keep people in their homes. As corporate auto racing promoter Roger Penske put it, "My biggest concern is that we've got to now focus on the neighborhoods. I see Bill Pulte Jr. is heading up a task force to tear down buildings. To me, you've got 80,000 derelict buildings and homes; once you take those down they won't be shelters for trouble." (Free Press 5/8/13.) People are being moved out of these neighborhoods not by use of eminent domain, but by foreclosures (mortgage or tax) and infamous water shutoffs, along with the systematic and *de facto* withdrawal of schools, churches, firehouses, and police stations. Some people just decide to move as it were. If you are willing, you don't have to look hard to see the racial dimensions of this new geography.

How does Belle Isle figure into these designs? How hard do you want to look?

PRIVATIZING THE COMMONS

First think for a moment about *Campus Martius,* in one sense Detroit's oldest park, the origin and intersection of the spoke street design created by Augustus Woodward after the big Detroit fire. In recent years the old name has been reclaimed. The park, like all of downtown, is under thorough electronic surveillance, fed to a control room not at police headquarters, but at Quicken Loans (also a major sponsor of Belle Isle events). It's patrolled by private security, also under Quicken's Dan Gilbert, with their own cars and sidearms. In summer, beach sand it brought in for volleyball and the outdoor bar serves a certain clientele craft beers and wine under the shade of wide umbrellas. The clientele is almost exclusively white. And they know the space is theirs.

My friend, Kim Redigan, tells how Women in Black, who vigil silently against war and the occupation of Palestine, had been ordered out of Campus Martius (as they had along the Riverwalk). They refused to obey. Two of their number filed suit with the help from the ACLU and prevailed, but first amendment rights are not to be presumed in privatized space. Last Good Friday, when our congregation again walked the streets of the city, pausing to pray at locations where crucifixion may be recognized today, an irate *Campus Martius* shop owner called the private cops when we gathered at the fountain to reflect on the Detroit water struggle. He expected that we could be simply driven off on command.

Remember that access to water figured into the civil rights struggle. Don't just picture "white" and "colored" over separate drinking fountains, think about public pools. The freedom struggle song, "If You Miss Me at the Back of the Bus . . ." has another verse that goes, "If you miss me at the swimmin' hole and you can't find me nowhere, come on over to the City Pool, I'll be swimmin' right there . . . ."

Now, picture water access on the Michigan coastline which has been black majority or safe home spaces for African Americans. Last year at a beach in Port Sanilac, up in the thumb, we had to complain to the DNR folks about small swastikas marked into the parking curb by the breakwater. If they hadn't been removed, we'd have done it ourselves, but that's about claiming "white space" where black folks are unwelcome, openly threatened, at risk.

One safe common place has been the waterfront in Benton Harbor, a black majority city on Lake Michigan with the lowest per capita income in the state. Jean Klock Park was given to the city for a park "in perpetuity." But as Whirlpool and the developers in St. Joseph coveted the entire lake- and riverfront, it became highly contested. Twenty two acres of wooded land at the center of the park were appropriated for three holes of a Jack Nicklaus golf course connected with a condominium village called Harbor Shores. Like virtually every other black city in Michigan, Benton Harbor is under emergency management. Rev. Edward Pinkney, who fought the expropriation, is doing three years hard time in state prison on set-up election fraud charges. At present the beach itself remains, but it is an island in the continuing upscale encroachment.

Maybe you want to press around Lake Michigan to Chicago's south side beaches, but if you stick with Michigan's coast, the only other place where a black majority city has this kind of water access is Belle Isle.

When the state took over the island last summer, one of the first things to happen was the dispatching of the integrated Detroit police force. They were replaced by state police (almost uniformly white) and DNR authorities (likewise). Moreover, they immediately began doing stops of vehicles for any sort of minor violation and checking the ID not just of the driver, but all occupants of the car. News stories tallied the arrests for child support, outstanding warrants, and the like. Never mind undocumented folks hearing loud and clear: don't take the chance just to enjoy wind and water. Even the mayor (well reported and probably staged) got pulled over, outraged, for speeding. The first three months, actually February through April, police reported fifty-five arrests from 329 traffic stops on the island.

As a state park, a prohibition against alcohol will now be enforced—at least "selectively." Ron Olson, chief of parks and recreation for the DNR, said up front there wouldn't be extreme enforcement of the no-alcohol policy—the idea is to prevent young people from having a beer party along the riverfront, but a couple enjoying some wine with their afternoon picnic will likely be left alone. (CBS Detroit 3/6/14.) Alcohol profiling.

As I write, it's Juneteenth weekend (and anniversary of the riots). I loop the island to check out the reunions on the third weekend in June. Lo and behold, turns out it's a day they're selling and checking passes at the gatehouse. Extended families are sparse under an overcast sky. I see a few with bright matching T-shirts. One pavilion is empty altogether. Not how I remember it. It's also the Fireworks and Freedom Festival weekend. Detroit youth are curfewed to their homes unless they have a note from their parents. Profiling and criminalizing is possible. The mayor actually wanted a standing ordinance, but faced with citizen outrage the council granted only the night of the big display.

Last fall a group of African American elders who for three decades have jogged the island together and now walk it, told Kim Redigan they were done. Not just because of age, but because they no longer feel welcome in their own place. In the parks of our church's own neighborhood, Corktown, benches have been removed, officially and unofficially, to prevent homeless people from resting their heads or otherwise feeling welcome.

Detroit filmmaker Kate Levy sends me a Facebook link to the latest corporate and conservancy video boosting island redevelopment (https://

vimeo.com/127904637). It begins with a mock scrapbook remembering the good old days. Ernest corporate and non-profit folks (all white) share their memories with grainy black-and-white images to confirm and assist. But then comes the full color future with formula one racers speeding away and young people exhilarated on their water boards. Bottom line: the corporations who do business in Detroit have a social responsibility, it's said, "to make Belle Isle become what it once was." In Detroit, that is a loaded and coded phrase. Listen for it. To what, precisely, is the city or its park coming "back?" How many decades do we have to go back to get there? The answer to that is actually pretty precise.

In the video Roger Penske speaks of the incredible decay the park suffered over the years. For what reason? Or at whose hands? Such questions would be better explored in depth than simply implied. His own solution has been to cover vast portions of the island's west end with a fourteen-inch slab of concrete. Since starting the engines in 2012, Penske and friends have invested $4.5 million repairing the 2.3-mile racetrack (Crains 5/6/15). Overall investment in the track area approaches $13 million. Other improvements include a world-class drainage system to keep the Grand Prix track runnable in rain, which actually doused it well a few weeks ago. Would that there were such sewage infrastructure improvements for the city as a whole, but the banks took that $500 million bond money right off the top on the interest rate swaps buy out.

I'm glad there are people who love the island and commit to its care. But conservancies are tricky things. I visit an island off the coast of RI where they protect pristine dune and marsh land from development. Good that. But the conservancy thereby increases the speculative value of the homes adjacent, already built. The wealthy love and support it. In Detroit, park conservancies function as extra-democratic fronts for corporate or foundation agendas. Which is to say, for privatization. The Belle Isle Conservancy is just now in the midst of a foundation-funded strategic planning process. Think of it as a well-funded closed-door conversation with corporate partners.

Already there is another summer car race slated for the island in July—the Red Bull Global Rallycross. It wasn't even on the calendar until a few weeks ago. Without any public meetings or hearings, it was simply announced by Red Bull. Another weekend of blocked access on the island. Moreover, Red Bull aspires, like Penske and Quicken, to be a major sponsor of island events, brokering projects already under review by the DNR.

Belle Isle has long been coveted by Detroit's big casinos. Originally they all built temporary ones, hoping for permanent homes on the island or the waterfront. The same may be said of hotel and restaurant operators. State management is little more than the mechanism for the great giveaway. Consider what a dozen years of state control have done for the privatization and decimation of education in Detroit. A developer has published a "novel" fantasizing a fully grown independent "commonwealth" (royally chartered?) on the island: hotels, quaint malls, a harbor, complete with residential spralls—a gated community with only one gate. Such extremes only serve to justify the lesser slips of the state-run slope. It is constantly denied that there are plans for a hotel on the island.

A PRAYER FOR LOVE HONORED

I know white people love Belle Isle. Part of me wants to honor that. In the promotional video, there is talk of turning sixteen, filling the car with gas, and coming to the island to drive round and round til the gauge read empty. A rite of passage. But somehow, it seems, this love is enhanced by covering the island with cement and running auto races upon it. The love I want to honor is felt at the family reunions and before the sacred trees. I think of runners and swimmers, safe and free in a place of their own. My heart yearns for the beat of soul, funk, and hip-hop concerts, where even as an outsider in my own skin, I find myself welcomed nonetheless.

I am at a loss. Can it be unpaved? Can the sacred trees and the groves rise again? Can memory be planted, sprouted, and nurtured? Can Manitou sing? Can the river wash us clean? Can *la frontera nortena* welcome us? Can the desecrated be resacralized? Can the corporations be stopped? Can white people notice what the hell they are doing and be saved by those they've dissed and buked? I'm trying not to doubt it. But the evidence goes against me. Against us all.

Nevertheless. This is a prayer to the One who flows around us, over us, in us. Come. Come in judgement and mercy. Come home like the sturgeon. Glide as a swan and strike. Slither like the snake unexpected. Re-engineer this world only as the beaver. Come as wild grass that grows through the cracks. Break from below the concrete idols. Dance on its rubble as at wedding. Grow like the truth at the poor one's door. Unite as all relations. Burst forth like the buried stream. Rage like a bridge afire. Let the gatehouse crumble. Let the governor and his petty minions fail. Let the cop cars stall and the guns go silent. Let the wounds release their victims. Set the bath house prisoners free. Let the invasive species wither at their roots. Let the island be sown or go feral with love. May the sacred commons spread. And yes, may the waters go round. Amen.

2016

The Jury is Still Out: The Last Vestige of Democracy

GEEZ MAGAZINE, MARCH 2016

The jury is still out on a case of Detroit water justice. In fact, by a circuit court judge's order, the jury has been sent indefinitely away.

A year ago, in July of 2014, when we were first charged for blocking the trucks of a private company hired to shut off water to some 3,000 homes a week, we demanded a jury trial. Detroit was under emergency management and every elected official in the city (as in every black city in the state) had been replaced by a single man appointed by the governor. In the manner of corporate fascism, he could set budgets, write ordinances, repeal laws, privatize departments, break union contracts, rewrite the city charter, declare bankruptcy, sell city assets like the water department, and order water shut off of anyone more than two months or $150 behind on their bill. A jury was the last vestige of democracy in the city. And we were bound to have them vote.

Two of us have now been through a trial filled with moving testimony. At the outset I told the jury: *what I would ask of you in these days at hand: keep your eyes open; keep your ears, your hearts, and your conscience open. Look for the meaning and spirit of these events. If you do that I will gladly put myself in your hands.* I believe they did just that.

But then. While we were making closing arguments, the Corporation Counsel of Detroit, the head of the law department, went secretly to the circuit court and got an emergency stay, pending a motion for mistrial. Apparently too much truth was in the air. Too many eyes and ears and hearts were open. After the jury heard all the evidence and arguments, after they had been charged and instructed, they were told to go home until further notice. No direct democracy needed here, thank you.

As to testimony: my codefendant was Marian Kramer. In Detroit, the water struggle is led substantially by strong black women. Mother Kramer is one of those. A veteran of the freedom struggle, and cochair of Michigan Welfare Rights Organization, she was a founder of the People's Water Board Coalition in 2000. I first met her when she was setting up a tent city on the lawn of the statehouse, and thereafter she invited me to join the panel of a truth commission about water in Detroit. Of course, in the trial, she took the stand in our behalf. She spoke with a moral force hard to silence with legal objections. Marian is one of my mentors in the ministries of social justice. I was honored to be on trial with her.

Another who testified was Monica Lewis-Patrick, spiritual thinker, founder of We The People of Detroit, who have set up water stations delivering over 10,000 gallons of water in the last year to shutoff victims. They run a hotline for the crisis and are in the midst of a sophisticated city mapping project which overlays tax and mortgage foreclosures, school closings, public health statistics, and arson—along with water shutoffs. Lo and behold it appears that as the city downsizes, privileging certain neighborhoods, that there are other neighborhoods, all black and poor, deemed to have futures only as green space for redevelopment. The shutoffs figure into this racial geography, expelling people from their homes and communities, threatening their elders with the emergency room and their children with Protective Services. Monica gets that 20 percent of the world's surface fresh water flows by this city and through our watershed. She understands that the corporations, knowing the imminence of water conflict, want to control it, even claim to "own it."

Others in the dock included Rev. JoAnn Watson, former councilwoman, who shepherded legislation for the "water affordability plan" a decade ago, never implemented, which would have set rates according to income. The city attorneys claim such an approach is illegal and unconstitutional. But Philadelphia is implementing just such a form of justice right now.

Attorney Alice Jennings testified to the civil rights case filed first in bankruptcy court (an emergency manager can also declare bankruptcy) and now in federal court on behalf of shutoff victims. Two of her plaintiffs also took the stand in our criminal case to tell the horrific and heroic stories of living without water. Such are the women warriors of the Detroit water movement.

I was allowed to question them all directly because I defended myself, speaking on my own behalf in the trial. That's unusual, but it is one's right. I generally find it humanizes a courtroom. Marian had a great attorney from the National Lawyers Guild. Yet someone not steeped or stilted in legal jargon and strictures can sometimes more readily bumble into truth in court. It meant I got to speak directly to the jury in opening and closing statements, but also when I put myself on the stand.

In the dock I recounted our action in detail, specifically telling its prayerful character. That day in July we shared water from a large chalice which sat for most of the trial on the defense table with an evidentiary number pasted to it. We variously drank from this vessel, poured libations, blessed one another—and from it drew a line of water the length of the driveway. I told about dedicating our action to Charity Hicks, who was the Rosa Parks of this water movement, jailed for resisting the shutoff of her neighbors' homes. She'd just then gone to the ancestors, struck in a suspicious hit-and-run accident. When the prosecutor objected, the judge asked me about the relevance of this fact. I answered that I considered her present as an eye witness. Said the judge, "In spirit you mean?" Yes. Indeed.

Though I wasn't allowed to enter it formally into evidence, I referenced a statement released the day prior to the action by National Nurses United, declaring a public health emergency in Detroit.

I also read from the letter that we delivered that morning to Homrich Inc., the private demolition company paid $5.2 million to do shutoffs, whose gates we blocked for seven and a half hours. It was signed by five bishops, and eighty local religious leaders and allies. It read, in part:

> In our traditions water is a free grace, part of the great gift that underlies all creation. We drink it as life itself. We wade through it to freedom. And in conversion we are immersed and sprinkled and cleansed. In season we know to honor it even by fasting from it. It is the lifeblood of the planet, circulating as rain and river. Water is the very emblem of the commons, what we hold together as one. We share it beholden to local indigenous peoples who understood, understand this deeply. For governments which serve the people, a water system is a public trust, held in trust for this generation and those to come. For the United Nations access to clean potable water is counted a human right.

Rejecting privatization outright, the letter called for an end to the shutoffs, for implementing the water affordability plan, and recognizing water as a human right.

In cross examination, the prosecutor asked if I thought Detroit Water and Sewage was on trial here. I paused. Yes, I said. She went ballistic telling the jury I was just using this courtroom for political theater. Frankly I thought in that moment of Jesus on trial before the authorities, albeit charged with refusing taxes to Caesar, foreseeing the destruction of the temple, declaring an alternative form of rule. He is asked, Are you then a messiah, a king? He replies, "Yes, and you shall see the Human Being seated at the right hand of power and coming on the clouds of heaven." They go ballistic. What other evidence do they need? Yet, everyone knows he's talking about another judgement which stands deeper just behind the present one. Truth be told, it's the high priest, the Sanhedrin, the Roman governor who are really on trial.

In my closing statement to the jury, I referenced the exchange with the prosecutor saying: I believe in this moment we are all on trial. What role are we going to play? How will we act in conscience?

At this writing we are still fighting legally to get things back to the jury and see what in conscience they say. The prosecutor fears it. The mayor and his corporation counsel fear it. But the people welcome it. May these citizens, our peers, be allowed to vote. Let justice come roll down like waters upon our city.

Bibliography

Balderrama, Francisco E., and Raymond Rodriguez. *Decade of Betrayal: Mexican Repatriation in the 1930s.* Albuquerque: University of New Mexico Press, 2006.
Boggs, Grace Lee. *The Next American Revolution: Sustainable Activism for the Twenty-First Century.* Berkeley, CA: University of California Press, 2011.
Conot, Robert. *American Odyssey.* Detroit: Wayne State University Press, 1986.
Cradle Will Rock. Dir. Tim Robbins. Touchstone Pictures. December 1999.
Dawn, Marva J. Sandberg. *The Concept of the "Principalities and Powers" in the Work of Jacques Ellul.* PhD diss., University of Notre Dame, 1992.
Delgado, Sharon. *Shaking the Gates of Hell: Faith-Led Resistance to Corporate Globalization* Minneapolis: Fortress, 2007.
Dillard, Angela D. *Faith in the City: Preaching Radical Social Change in Detroit.* Ann Arbor, MI: University of Michigan Press, 2007.
Ellul, Jacques. *The Meaning of the City.* Grand Rapids: Eerdmans, 1970.
Forgotten: The Murder at the Ford Rouge Plant, a Jazz Opera. Music and lyrics by Steve Jones, 2003.
Frida. Dir. Julie Taymor. Lions Gate Films. August 2002.
Fullilove, Mindy Thompson. *Root Shock: How Tearing Up City Neighborhoods Hurts America, and What We Can Do About It.* New York: Ballantine, 2005.
Gornik, Mark. *To Live in Peace: Biblical Faith and the Changing Inner City.* Grand Rapids: Eerdmans, 2002.
Grandin, Greg. *Fordlandia: The Rise and Fall of Henry Ford's Forgotten Jungle City.* New York: Metropolitan, 2009.
Georgakas, Dan, and Marvin Surkin. *Detroit: I Do Mind Dying.* Cambridge, MA: South End, 1998.
Hendrickson, Wilma, ed. *Detroit Perspectives: Crossroads and Turning Points.* Detroit: Wayne State University Press, 1991.
Hopkins, Dwight. "The Religion of Globalization." In *Religions/Globalizations,* edited by Dwight Hopkins et al., 7–32. Durham, NC: Duke University Press, 2001.
Mast, Robert H., ed. *Detroit Lives.* Philadelphia: Temple University Press, 1994.
Rodrigues, Michael, and Thomas Featherstone. *Detroit's Belle Isle: Island Park Gem.* Charleston, SC: Arcadia, 2003.

Saunders, Stanley P., and Charles Campbell. *The Word on the Street.* Grand Rapids: Eerdmans, 2000.

Sugrue, Thomas J. *The Origins of the Urban Crisis: Race and Inequality in Postwar Detroit.* Princeton, NJ: Princeton University Press, 1996.

Stringfellow, William. *A Keeper of the Word: Selected Writings of William Stringfellow*, edited by and with an introduction by Bill Wylie-Kellermann. Grand Rapids: Eerdmans, 1994.

———. *William Stringfellow: Essential Writings.* Selected with an introduction by Bill Wylie-Kellermann. Maryknoll, NY: Orbis, 2013

Wink, Walter, *Unmasking the Powers.* Philadelphia: Fortress Press, 1987.

Wylie-Kellermann, Bill. *Seasons of Faith and Conscience: Kairos, Confession, Liturgy.* Maryknoll, NY: Orbis, 1991. 2nd edition with a new introduction. Eugene, OR: Wipf and Stock, 2009.

———"Unions and Communities." *Boston Review*, XXI (Summer 1996) 17.

Wylie, Jeanie. *Poletown: Community Betrayed.* Urbana, IL: University of Illinois Press, 1989.

Subject Index

AFL-CIO, 27
Allied Media Conference, 55
Allinsky, Saul, 77
Ambassador Bridge, 61, 123
Anderson, Rhonda, xi, 146
Angel, of Detroit, 1, 10, 12, 49, 51; of nations, 3; of Jerusalem, 4, 5;
Anishinaabe, xviii, 120, 141
Archdiocese of Detroit, 18, 73, 93, 143
Arab Community, 5, 59
Arson, 9, 21, 22, 129, 154
Associated Press, 17
Authorities, 115; Detroit Blight Removal Authority, 131; Educational Achievement Authority (EAA), 115; Great Lakes Water Authority (GLWA), 116

Babel, 4, 8, 11, 60
Banks, 100; Bank of America, 88, 92, 93, 96, 100 108; J.P. Morgan Chase, 66
Barlowe, Maude, 107; and Council of Canadians, 108
Basketball, xxvii, 31–37
Beaupre, Shirley, 126
BeeHive Design Collective, xvii
Beloved Community, xiii, 59, 76, 77, 101, 106, 132
Bennett, Harry, xxix, 42, 63, 65

Belle Isle, xix, xxiv, xxviii, 6, 139–52; 141; conservancy, 149, 152; and the "healing tree," 146; as "Hog Island," 142; as *Wahnabeezee* (Swan Island), 142
Berrigan, Daniel, xiii, 81, 84
Berrigan, Phillip, 90
Bing, Mayor David, 67, 74, 92, 94, 130
Black Bottom, 74, 125, 144
Blockbusting, 20, 129
Bloody Run Stream, 136
Bobb, EFM Robert, 113
Boggs, Grace Lee, xiii, xv, xxv, 26, 28, 134
Boggs, Jimmy, xiii, 146
Boggs Center for Community Leadership, xv
Bradford, Rev. Lewis, xix, 40–42
Brown vs. Kansas Board of Education, 28, 112

Casinos, 1, 16, 38, 49, 51, 86, 151
Cass Corridor, 6, 20, 123, 124
Cass, General Lewis, 124
Catholic Worker, 41, 42, 89, 105, 120; Detroit, xi, xv, xxvii, 13, 31, 51, 92, 94, 120, 132, 137
Charles Wright Museum of African American History, 80
Christian Community Development Association, 75

Churches, xxi, xxv, xxvii, 3, 5, 11, 17, 18, 20, 32, 47, 62, 75, 77 fn. 9, 81, 101, 102, 121, 124; anti-church, 57; Central United Methodist, 40; church closings, 74–75, 94, 130, 146; Immaculate Conception Church, 17–18, 74; as place-based, xxiii, 71–78; Riverside Church, 33; Spirit of Hope, 36; and white flight, 75; See also St. Peter's Episcopal Church

Climate change, 43

Columbus, Christopher, 14

Commodity fetishism, 64

Conservancy, 122, 150

Corktown, 68, 120, 149; and "Conquistadors," 121–23, 132; and subsidized housing, 126; and Urban Renewal, 125

Corporations, xx, xxiv, xxvii, 9, 12, 19, 26, 28, 73, 77, 88, 90, 93, 112, 115, 123, 125, 150, 151, 154

Covington, Chancellor John, 116

Coughlin, Father Charles, 42, 64, 143–44

Crack houses, 10–11, 20, 21, 22

Curtis, Kezia, xii

Day, Dorothy, 41

Davis, Pablo, 59, 64

Detroit, as Arsenal of Democracy, 51, 62, 144; and bankruptcy, 90, 93–96, 100, 113, 153; as Black majority city, 139; as blank slate, 77; as Cuba of the Rustbelt, 54; and deindustrialization, 54, 56; as *de troit* ("the straits"), 6, 15, 50, 76, 142; and downsizing, 115; and food security, 53; and home-owning, 91, 129; as Motor City, 52; as "Murder City," 3, 25, 145; as vacant land, 52

Detroit Black Community Food Security Network, 53

Detroit Coalition Against Police Brutality, 69; and Peace Zones for Life, 69, 79

Detroit Economic Growth Corporation, 22, 121, 128

Detroit Free Press, 26, 115

Detroit Future City Mapping, 130, 147

Detroit Independent Free School Movement, xii

Detroit Industrial Murals, xiii, 56–65, *See also* Diego Rivera

Detroit Institute of Arts, 57

Detroit MetroTimes, xxvii, 31, 116

Detroit Newspaper strike, xxvi, 24–30,

Detroit News, 24, 26; editor Nolan Finley, 128

Detroit Peace Community, xi

Detroit Peoples' Water Board Coalition, 107, 154

Detroit School Board, elected, 86, 119; in exile, 114, 125;

Detroit Race Riot of 1943, 143–45

Detroit Renaissance Center, 6, 8, 60

Detroit Rebellion of 1967, xxiii, 81, 128, 145

Detroit River, xii, 15, 46, 60, 76, 110; and ancient sturgeon, 141

Detroit Sunday Journal, 29

Detroit Water and Sewage Department, xxvii, 6, 92, 105, 108, 110, 116; on trial, 156

Detroit Water Struggle, xxviii, 102–11, 148

Detroiters Resisting Emergency Management, xiii, 139

Duggan, Mayor Michael, 87, 90, 92, 109, 119, 128, 130, 149, 156

Duncan, Charles, 68

Economics, casino, 16, 38, 50; community-based, 19, 23, 52–55, 72; disaster capitalism,

91, 113; global, 38; manna-gift, 137; service-based, 39
Edison, Thomas, 61, 62
Electric Park, 143
Ellul, Jacques, 1, 3–4, 8
Elmwood Cemetery, 6, 76, 136
Emergency Management, xx, xxiv, xxvii, 82, 87, 89–95, 106, 109, 112, 114, 119, 125, 128, 139, 148; and bankruptcy, 90, 154, 92, 93, 96, 97; defined, 88, 139, 153; and participatory democracy, 72, 83; and schools, 87, 92, 112, 113, 114, 116, 125; and water, xxvii, 106, 109, 110, 111; and white racism, xxvii, 82, 90, 148, 153
Empire, xxv, 14, 55, 60, 73, 78, 81, 98, 135, 137
Engler, Governor John, 112
Exorcism, 11, 98

Farm Labor Organizing Committee (FLOC), 66
Fellowship of Reconciliation, 41
Ford, Henry, 41, 42, 59, 60–64, and Hitler, 62
Ford, Glenn, 93
Ford Hunger March, 42, 58, 143
Ford Rouge Plant, xxvi, 40, 52, 56, 57, 58, 59, 60, 63, 64, 157
Fordlandia, 61, 62 fn. 4
Foreclosures, 50, 67, 82, 91, 100, 107, 115, 129, 130, 131, 147, 154
Forgotten, jazz musical, xxvi, 40–42
Fullilove, Mindy, 73, 146

Gandhi, Mohandas, xxiii, 40, 81
General Motors, 9, 17–18, 22, 74
Gentrification, 95, 103, 120–33; defined, 127; Detroit style, 128, 130
Gilbert, Dan, 127, 131, 147; and Quicken Loans, 126, 128, 147, 150
Great Depression, 40, 58, 125, 143 and Hoovervilles, 40, 143

Greensboro Community Truth and Reconciliation Project, 106
Griebler, Denise xi, xii, xiii, xiv, 63
Groan, xxv, 57, 60
Gumbleton, Bishop Thomas, 30
Guyette, Kurt, xiv, 116
Guyton, Tyree, 54

Harris, Brooke, 117
Hastings Street, 125, 144, 147. *See also* Black Bottom and Paradise Valley
Heidelberg Project, 54
Herrada, Elena, xii, 58, 58 fn. 3, 83, 86, 97; *See also* Detroit School Board in exile
Herrada, Jose Santos, 58, 59
Hicks, Charity, xi, xii, xv, xix, xxv, xxvii, xxix, 102, 137, 155; and "Wage Love," 102, 104, 106, 109
Hitler, Adolph, 41, 62, 144
Homrich Wrecking, Inc., 108, 155
Homrich 9, xii, 153, 156
House, Gloria Aneb, xi, xii, xix
Howell, Shea, xii, xiv, 146
Hurricane Katrina, 113

Immigration and Customs Enforcement (ICE), 47, 59, 61; and the Ku Klux Klan, 47
Indigenous peoples, 15, 60, 62, 76, 124, 141–42

Jackson, President Andrew, 124
Jails, Detroit Central Detention, 103, 105; D.C. City, 34; Macomb Co., 34; Oakland Co., 34, 81
Jennings, Alice, xi, xii, 154
Jesus, 6, 10, 27, 43, 70, 138, and the bank, 99, 100; his body, 98; or the church, 140; confronting the city, 4; crucified, 13, 70, 77; discerning the angel of Jerusalem, 4, 5; on the march, xxv; resisting violence and empire, 81; on trial, 156

Subject Index

Johnson, Nelson and Joyce, xii, 106, 107, 109
Jones, Councilwoman Brenda, 82
Jones-Day, law firm, 81, 84, 87, 93, 96, 101
Jones, Prophet, 146
Jones, Steve, xxvi, 41, 42
Juneteenth, 144, 146, 149
Jury, nullification, 84, 156; as last vestige of democracy, 83, 94, 97, 153–54

Kahn, Albert, 127
Kairos, xxv, 4, 5
Keepers of the Mountain, West Virginia, 108
Kern, Father Clem, 70, 126
King, Martin Luther, Jr., 5, 58, 81, 82, 94, 124
Kramer, Marian, xi, xii, 154, 155
Ku Klux Klan, 47, 106

Land, urban clearing, xxvi, 67, 115, 126, 130–31; and eminent domain, 130
Lee, Spike, 128
Lester, Muriel, 41
Levy, Kate, xiii, 115, 127, 149
Lewis-Patrick, Monica xi, 154

Mangrum, Father John, 126
Manna, 55, 137–38; Community Garden, 137, 138;Community Meal, 68, 120, 123, 137
Maroon, Matty, 123
Marshall, Thurgood, 145
Martin, B. Herbert, 78
Martin, Trayvon, 70
Mast, Robert, xxvi
Maurin, Peter, 41, 89, 92
Media, Detroit, xxiv, 22, 26, 55, 72, 82, 87, 90, 127, 149; national, 22. *See also: Associated Press, Detroit Free Press. Detroit News, Detroit MetroTimes, Michigan Citizen*

Merton, Thomas, 45
Mexican Repatriation, 58, 58 fn. 3, 125
Michigan Central Station, train, 122, 123, 137
Michigan Citizen, xiv, 40 fn.2, editor, Terry Kelley, xiv
Michigan Welfare Rights Organization, 123, 153
Mitchel, Robert "Tazzy," 68
Mitchell, Joni, 79
Moore, Helen, xi, 112,
Moral Monday's Movement, 106, 108
Moten, Emmett, 20

National Lawyers Guild, xii, 155
National Nurses United, 108, 155
New Detroit, 132
New Orleans, 91, 106, 113, 119
Nonviolence, xxi, xxvi, 12, 18, 30–31, 49, 81, 87, 97, 140
North American Free Trade Agreement (NAFTA), xviii, 47, 61

Ogemawke, Chief, 124
Olmstead, Frederick Law, 143
Orr, Kevyn, 82, 88, 93, 96, 139

Paradise Valley, 74, 126, 144, 147
Penske, Roger, 139, 147, 150
Peoples' Affordability Plan of 2005, 107, 109, 111, 154, 156
Perkinson, Jim, xii, xxv
Pinkney, Rev. Edward, 148
Poletown 9, 18, 19; book, 158; documentary, xxvi, 18, 20, 130; plant 18, 52, 74
Pontiac, Chief, 136, 142
Principalities and Powers, xiv, xvii, xxvii, 2, 3, 4, 9, 13, 14, 15, 24, 26, 27, 41, 42, 51, 63, 76, 78, 115

Quicken Loans, *See* Dan Gilbert

Readers United (RU), xii, xxvii, 25, 27–30
Redigan, Kim, xi, xii, 148, 149
Redlining, 129
Restrictive covenants, 129
Rivera, Diego, xiii, xix, xxvi, 6, 42, 56, 58, 59, 61, 60, 62, 63, 64
Rhodes, Steven, 96
Roberts, EM Roy, 115
Rodriguez, Sixto, 123

Save Our Sons and Daughters (SOSAD), 21, 146
Schools, Catherine Ferguson Academy, 53; charter, xx, 87, 92, 113, 114, 115, 118, 119; Cooley High School, xxiii, 31, 32, 34, 81, 129; Ethelyn Crockett Academy, 125; Finney High School, 125; Henry Ford High School, 33; Barbara Jordon Academy, 125; Oakman Orthopedic, 114, 115; theological, xiv
Scott, James, fountain, 141
Shakour, Satori, 80
Snyder, Governor Rick, xx, 92, 93, 106, 111, 113, 116, 131, 139. 142, 151
Spirit of Detroit sculpture, xxv, 7, 21
St. Peter's Episcopal Church, xx, xxviii, 51, 78, 92, 94, 97, 106, 120, 122, 126, 132, 137, 139; on the market, 120: and subsidized housing policy, 126; as water distribution station, 108
Stations of the Cross, xx, xxvii, 13, 15, 16, 38, 43, 44, 47, 51, 58, 66, 68, 70, 77, 77 fn. 9, 98, 100
Stringfellow, William, xiii, 4
Stop the Robberies, Enjoy Safe Streets (STRESS), 145
Structural adjustment, xviii, 91, 113, 119
Surveillance, 46, 63, 63 fn. 5, 92, 94, 147

Teach for America, 118–19
Tiger Stadium, 5, 38, 39, 52, 121, 127

United Auto Workers (UAW), 51, 108
United Nations, 45, 102, 107, 110, 155; Special Rapporteurs on Water and Housing, 111
United States Social Forum, xvii, xxvi, 55, 56, 136
United States, Department of Defense, 43; Department of Homeland Security 47, 61, 63 fn. 5

Vance Security, 29
Vocation, xi, xxiii, 3, 4, 24–25, 27–29, 41, 52, 76, 118
Voting Rights Act, 89, 92

Water, affordability, 46, 107, 153, *See also* Peoples Water Affordability Plan of 2005; commodification, 45, 107; as commons, 107; in Freedom Struggle, 148; as human right, 44, 102, 107, 110, 111, 131, 137, 155–56; and public health, 108, 154–55; as public trust, 107, 110; as sacred gift, 107, 155; shut-offs, 44, 102, 105, 106, 108, 115, 120, 131, 153; and watershed, 141, 154
Watershed discipleship, xxv, 76
Watson, JoAnn, minister and Councilwoman, xi, xiv, 82, 84, 91, 154
Wawiatanong, xviii, 15, 76, 141
We the People of Detroit, 108, 154
We the People Reclaiming Our Streets (WEPROS), 20
White Flight, 75, 91; as organized and engineered, xvii, 50, 62, 65, 128–129
Wilderness, 47, 55, 60, 137
Williams, Charles II, xiv, 83
Wink, Walter, xiii, 4

Women in Black, 148
Woodward, Augustus, 147
Wylie-Kellermann, Bill, xix, xvi, xx, 17–23, 77 fn. 9, 87, 96–97, 102
Wylie-Kellermann, Jeanie xi, xiv, xxvi, xxvii, 17–23, 24, 31, 35, 81, 141

Young, Mayor Coleman Alexander, 2, 50, 145

Zapatistas, 72
Zelinsky, Mike, xii

www.ingramcontent.com/pod-product-compliance
Lightning Source LLC
Chambersburg PA
CBHW031433150426
43191CB00006B/494